THE PROPERTY COACH

THE PROPERTY COACH

Property investing at its very best

Aran Curry

The Insight Group

The Insight Group
Enterprise Centre
Auborough Street
Scarborough
YO11 1HT
www.propertyinsight.info
info@theinsightgroup.co.uk

Published by The Insight Group
©Copyright 2012 Aran Curry

We hope you enjoy this book and welcome any comments.

50% of all profits from this book are given to charity to help those in debt; thank you so much for your contribution.

Order this book online at:
www.propertyinsight.info/buybooknow/

And you can access your bonus material here:
www.propertyinsight.info/bonusmaterial/

In accordance with the Legal Deposit Libraries Act 2003 a copy of this book has been deposited with the British Library.

This book aims to provide accurate and authoritative information relating to the topics discussed. Neither the author nor the publisher can be held responsible for information that changes or for the actions of the reader.

ISBN: 978-0-9572202-0-1

Edited by Rupert Waddington

Short Run Press, Exeter, all materials FSC Mix accredited

For Leila, my inspiration and purpose, and Adam, Josh, Georgia and Sophie who light up my life in so many ways.

And for all those struggling with debt and poverty for whom the idea of investing, or even just buying this book, is out of reach.

Introduction

I am passionate about property – not the bricks and mortar but the income that property can generate and the time this can free up. People invest for many reasons but it's usually because of what the money earned can do, not for the money itself. And for this reason, property is a superb long-term investment with the capacity to generate large and sustainable incomes which open up new life choices.

I'm fortunate; I've been able to direct this passion into not one but several enterprises. I've spent 16 years developing my own property portfolio – and now, along with my teams, I provide many expert services for other property investors. You see, it really is a passion! But there's another dimension to it: helping people to find out for themselves how they want to develop their own property portfolio and invest for their future. And that's where this book comes in.

This is not a D.I.Y. book but a serious introduction to serious investing. Whilst written with business owners in mind, it is just as helpful for anyone with the drive and ability to achieve financial freedom. From tenants to tax, it covers all the topics you'll need to master, and gives advice on everything from valuing a property to finding the perfect plumber. In other words, it shows you 'how it all works'; you can then decide exactly what approach is right for you and which aspects you want more help with.

Of course there is a wealth of other information out there – at Property Insight, for example, we run investor events and produce regular newsletters. And if this book encourages you to explore those as well, or to take your own first step as investors, it has done what it set out to do. But above all, I hope the book lets you share my huge enthusiasm for property investing and convinces you that it is do-able, enjoyable and extremely profitable.

Happy reading – and happy investing.

Aran Curry

Why 'Property Coach'?

Earlier in my career I experienced the fantastic benefits of working with an expert business coach, learning skills that still serve me today as an investor and advisor. A coach doesn't just hold your hand while you develop your business, but helps you to think through your plans before putting them into action. And that's why this book introduces you to the fictional characters, Steve and Carol. They are new to investing and are attending a series of sessions with their own property coach. So, while you read, you can learn from them as they confront their own ambitions and fears and prepare to take their first steps as successful investors.

Contents

1. A chance encounter

"Damn!"

Steve bent forwards, his hands on his knees as he caught his breath. He'd been running to catch the 17:46 but now stood watching the train's tail lights disappear into the fog at the end of the platform. Both of his vans were out that day and, with the child minder ill, Carol was using the car for the school run. So today he'd travelled by train, something he rarely did but quite enjoyed. Now, however, he was tired and just wanted to get home. He checked his watch; nearly half an hour until the next train, just time for a quick drink. And hell, he'd earned it. The meeting had been a success, a renewal of an annual contract worth several thousands. Steve smiled; thank God, even in the digital age, people still wanted things printed on real paper.

He looked around the cold station concourse. At the far corner stood a tatty looking pub, the glow of red lamps beckoning travellers from behind its frosted glass. Steve went inside, ordered a pint and some peanuts and scoured the room for a spare table.

"Hey, Steve!" Hearing his name he turned round and saw a tall, fit man waving a newspaper in the air. He was casually but expensively dressed, with the glint of a slim gold watch and a deep tan emerging from a crisp double-cuffed shirt.

"Phil, what a surprise. It's been … how long?" They shook hands enthusiastically, old friends from some twenty years earlier. When they'd first met at Technical College they were rivals, each launching a new printing business. However they had quickly become allies, sitting at the back and passing notes during the less interesting classes. "Mind if I join you?"

"Of course not." He pulled out a chair for Steve. "So, what brings you into town?"

Steve ran through a brief summary of his day. Phil was impressed. "Sounds like business is going well then? And how's Carol? Last thing I heard she was expecting again. Your third isn't it?"

"Wow, that shows how long it's been," Steve smiled. "My youngest has just turned seven!"

Time passed quickly as they reminisced and, glancing at his watch, Steve saw he was just about to miss another train. So far he'd been doing most of the talking; he still hadn't heard how Phil's own business was going. Making a quick call home, he explained the situation. "Don't worry, it's only take-away tonight," Carol had replied, granting him leave to stay a little longer.

"Well Phil, I have to say, you look fantastic; rich and relaxed, a real advertisement for good living!" Phil smiled but didn't blush. He knew he'd done well and didn't mind other people knowing it. "I remember you had ambitious plans back then; millionaire by thirty-five, retired by forty. Tell me, what's actually happened?"

So Phil did. He told him how he'd missed the first goal by only one year, and then thought about retiring but found he wasn't ready to let go of the business just yet. Steve looked at him, not sure if he was being serious. Phil explained.

"It's all quite simple – I've been investing for the past few years and only last month my accountant showed me the results in black and white; the value of my investment assets – and that's after deducting outstanding mortgages – is now well over a million pounds."

"Wow!" Steve was impressed. "So why don't you retire? Ah … hang on, I know; you've used equity in the business to make the investments, that's it isn't it? I'm no Donald Trump but even I know that's dodgy – you could lose the lot!"

Phil laughed. "Of course not; nothing touches my business. No, I did release some equity in my house, but just enough to get started. And now I could repay that today if I wanted, so my home is secure just like the business. Tell you what though, I'll admit I've used some of the new money to bring in extra staff. No point working seven-day weeks now I don't have to!"

Steve sighed. "I'm impressed, but you should be talking to Carol. She always used to go on about investing – stuff she got off the internet, buying holiday blocks in Bulgaria or Spain, you know the kind of thing. I told her they're all get-rich-quick schemes for mugs so she's now started dragging me off to see IFAs[1] and to go to networking meetings." He grimaced at the thought of it.

Phil laughed again. "I remember you at College, always some excuse to miss the financial seminars – you just wanted to get on with the nitty gritty of the business."

"Yeah well, thank goodness Carol keeps a keen eye on the money. But I must say, even I am getting a bit worried; I mean, you know, we're doing OK – strong business, good clients – and I reckon that together we bring home about £60,000 a year. We've got a small pension, had one from the start – oh, and a flat in Leeds we rent out, but that's more an investment for the children really; do you know, we actually lose £50 a month on it? But I guess it's going up in value—"

....

1   Independent Financial Advisor

"A flat?" Phil interrupted. "New build?" he added. Steve nodded. "Hmm, you should look into that; not always the best property to put money into. Anyway," he saw Steve's look of concern, "sorry, you were saying …"

"Well, we know we should be saving more and planning for the future; and to be honest, I'm not sure I want to keep going at this rate until we retire – do you know it must be months since we were both able to spend a whole weekend together? I bet you don't have that problem!"

Phil smiled, thinking of his typical weekends – golf, sailing, city breaks – and asked, "Are you getting any help, you know, financial planning, that kind of thing?"

"We get loads of information but no real help." Phil looked puzzled at this so Steve explained. They'd gone round endless financial advisors, pension fund managers and investment specialists, each of whom had plenty of information to hand over, but no time to mentor or guide them through the actual process of putting their investment money to work.

"They make it all sound so complicated, and with all their jargon – I just switch off. And let's face it," Steve added, "even on our modest scale, any investment nowadays just seems so dangerous – what with stagnant interest rates and crumbling banks. How can you possibly trust someone with your money?"

"You can't." Phil replied bluntly. Steve was taken aback. "What I mean is, you're right; ultimately it has to be your own decision. But you can get help; you don't have to do it alone. Start by choosing the right investment – and then get yourself a coach. It's what I did."

"Sounds expensive to me! And anyway, we've always managed to do things ourselves; in fact it's something we're really proud of, learning the ropes, making mistakes, and still here, running a successful business—"

"And working bloody hard by the sound of it," Phil joked. "Seems you've forgotten one of the golden rules of growing an enterprise – don't be too proud to pay for expertise."

"Huh, all very well if you can afford it!" replied Steve.

"Speculate to accumulate, old friend! But actually, paying for a coach isn't speculating. Think of it instead as employing a specialist – and only for as long as you need. You work out where you want to go, the coach helps you find the best route, and within no time you're well on the way. And you're not making any expensive mistakes en route either."

Steve looked straight at Phil. It reminded him of Carol's friend who had turned around a failing business with the help of an advisor. The only reason they hadn't looked into it was because their own business was doing fine. They'd never thought of coaching in relation to saving and investing. And anyway, he'd always thought of it in relation to Life Coaching, help for people whose personal life was a disaster. But maybe Phil was onto something.

"So, if you had to get a coach, was that because your business was struggling?" Looking at his friend sitting opposite, it was hard to imagine he had ever hit bad times.

"No, not at all. Far from it, business was great. But like you two, I had an eye on the future, and it was beginning to look pretty unattractive – non-stop hard slog followed either by an early death from exhaustion or my twilight years surviving on a shrinking pension. And now I think about it, if I had a family like you I'd be even more determined to free up time and money while I'm still able to enjoy it."

Now Steve was growing confused. If the business was such a success, why did Phil need a coach?

"Property." Phil explained, "I went to a property coach, someone I'd met a few years before at a networking event. He'd given me his card along with a sheet of some pretty impressive figures and something made me file them away. I'm glad I did because one Sunday morning not long after, I was getting ready to go in and do a stock-check and I just knew, there and then, it had to change."

"Property eh?" Steve was curious. "You must be one tough landlord if it pays for things like that!" He pointed towards Phil's expensive watch.

"Well, I'd always thought of property – I think it's because you can actually see where your money is, feel you've got more control. But thank goodness I used a coach. Otherwise I'd have bought half a dozen new build flats in Leeds!"

That comment hit home hard but Steve was now completely hooked and keen to hear more.

"So, what did you do? How did you get started?"

"What I didn't do was just go out there and buy up houses. I first had to learn how it all works and my coach taught me – and then guided me through my first few purchases." Phil could see in Steve's eye the glint of serious interest. "Look, let me get you another drink and then I'll explain it all to you."

"No, this one's on me. But I'd better just call Carol again – and then the first question I'm going to ask is 'why property?'"

2. Why property?

Steve asks, "Why property?" It's an obvious question and the answer is very simple as I'll show in a moment. But first, I want to ask a different question – why *invest*?

Why invest?

> *We always overestimate the change that will occur in the next two years and underestimate the change that will occur in the next ten. Don't let yourself be lulled into inaction.*
>
> Bill Gates

Basically if you want financial freedom in the future, you can't afford *not* to invest. But investment, for many people, has simply never been on the radar. And it's not their fault; the traditional National Insurance and pension structures that we've all grown up with have made us feel safe, looked after and with our financial futures all planned for. But of course, more recently this has all been shaken to its foundations. Now more than ever, as I'll show in a moment, relying on pensions is a mistake.

But there are also other reasons why people don't invest. Some have a perception that only really wealthy people have investments and this is nonsense, as this book will show. Also, people mistakenly think that investing is always very complex and high-risk. My world, the world of Property Investing, is extremely well established. It's run by, and for, people like you and me, ordinary people who want to take control of their finances by investing in a future of financial freedom. All it takes is the right attitude, the right knowledge and the right help.

Can't I just rely on my pension?

To be blunt the answer is 'no', and for a number of reasons. Firstly, we have an increasing elderly population and as a result, the country faces an ever-larger pension bill. It is you and I who are paying this bill as we continue to work and pay taxes. And in the future we will have to work for longer in order to pay for our own retirement.

Another reason is that pension funds are often linked to the stock market *(figure 1)*, and the amount you receive at the end is dependent on how the market is performing at that time. If it's performing well, you may get a good pension for the rest of your life. But if it's *not,* then your pension is fixed for ever more at a lower rate! Effectively, people are gambling on this end figure but without having any control over it whatsoever.

Another wake-up call is that many private pension schemes can, and *have*, gone bust in recent years. An employee who's

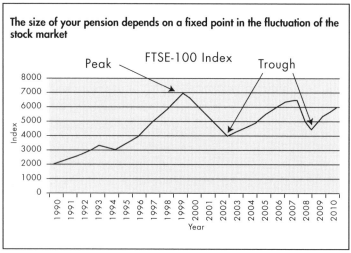

figure 1

worked for twenty years, expecting their pension to be safe, can suddenly find their financial situation has completely changed. And while there are some schemes in place to protect you against this, they rarely protect you fully and often leave people with less than they were expecting.

What about an annuity?

Buying an annuity is a way of investing the lump sum of your pension when you retire. Basically it's an agreement between you and an insurance company, securing a monthly income for the rest of your life. However, you need to understand what size of lump sum is needed to generate this desired income. Using an income target of £30,000 a year, *figure 2* shows how much this has changed over time, and especially in just the four years from 2008 to 2012.

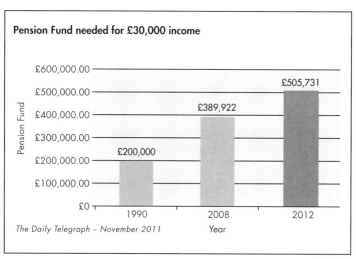

figure 2

And now, based on the 2012 figure of a £500,000 lump sum, see how much you have to save each month over three different periods to accrue that sum *(figure 3)*:

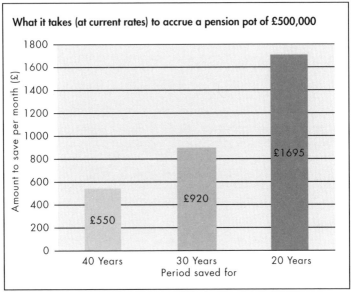

figure 3

Why learning to invest properly is crucial

Compared to this very gloomy scenario, investments can offer a much brighter future. But it's really important to choose the *right* investment by basing it on the return it gives you. For example, simply comparing a 2% and a 6% return, look at the difference over a 40 year period *(figure 4)*:

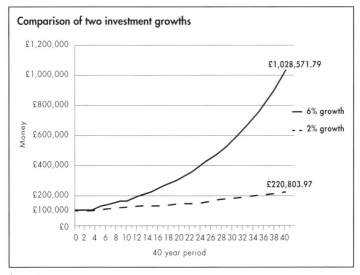

figure 4

You can see how just a 4% *difference* in growth returns can make a huge impact when you come to retire. This shows, in the clearest possible way, why it's so important to make sure your investments are getting you the best return.

Why property?

Before going into property in detail, I just want to be absolutely clear that becoming a property investor does *not* mean having to give up your job or selling your business. Of course you can exchange your current work with the full-time running of your portfolio, or you can use the available services and experts to do it all for you. And in chapter 3, the first coaching session, we'll meet two very ordinary people who run a successful business and have a family. We'll watch as they learn how to become investors *in addition* to everything they already do in their busy lives. Whichever route *you* choose, however, your financial security will no longer be totally dependent on your business or on the government or your pension fund.

So, why property? Well, let's take a 'true or false?' test.

1. Property investing is a reliable way of investing – *true or false?*

True: a survey of house price data shows clearly why property has always been a solid investment. If we look over the past eighty years, prices have gone up on average 7.9% each year. Look just at the last forty years, and that figure changes to an average of 10.3% per annum! *Figure 5* below shows growth since the late 1960s:

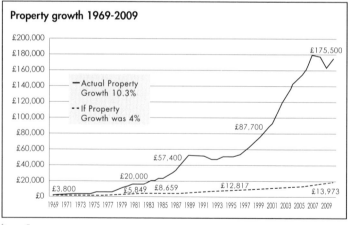

figure 5

Even during the last decade, when everyone says the housing market has been a real mess, prices have risen every year except two. And over the last ten years prices have still doubled. So it remains a steady climber, exactly what you need for a long-term investment.

2. Stocks and shares make a better investment – *true or false?*

False: traditionally the stock market has climbed and been a good investment. But take another look at the first graph (*figure 1*) showing pensions in relation to the stock market; it shows how, over a twelve year period, the value of the FTSE 100[2] *fell* by 20%. Against this, the 'stagnating' property market still doubled in value in ten years. The stock market can certainly offer good investments but it's wise to spread your risks, and property has definitely been a better average performer. Also, you can fund most of your property investment with a mortgage rather than personal finance. The only way to do the same on the stock market is through trading options, which require massive expertise.

3. Property investment is a high-performance investment – *true or false?*

True: it's not just because property value has always grown so reliably, but also because the property investment model is one that mushrooms. If you stick your money in a high-interest account, you hope to pull in reliable, fairly constant interest payments. But if you stick the same amount of money into a property portfolio, over time your portfolio grows and with each new property you multiply the return from your original investment. It's like putting it in the high-interest account but

....

2 Financial Times and London Stock Exchange figures showing the average price of the top 100 companies in the UK

seeing the interest payments double every few years, and double again, and again – something that of course will never happen in any bank account!

4. Property investment is becoming riskier – *true or false?*

False: it's easy to understand why people worry about this. Just because we've had an impressive 10%+ growth over the past four decades, will the future be as good? Will property continue to be something we can rely on? Well, certainly, we are living in a time of massive financial change. But I suggest a bit of lateral thinking, because however bad the economy in a country becomes, the housing market will respond in a unique way based on *real need* rather than on the whims of a small number of incredibly wealthy bankers and business-people.

Think about it; there is a housing shortage in the UK, and always will be. With immigration, rising divorce, people living longer and all the other factors making the population grow, we simply can't keep up with the increasing demand. If you don't believe me, look at the figures: the government statistics for 2012 show that we are already *one million* houses short and need 250,000 extra houses per annum to be built, but currently there are plans for only 120,000. Give it a few more years and that gap will be even bigger. And the one thing that maintains value for any commodity is demand outstripping supply.

Remember though that I'm talking about a long-term investment, not a get-rich-quick scheme, and you need to be comfortable knowing that year on year there will be downs as well as ups. And this is why all of my projections are based on a very conservative 4-5% – you'll find the same in the coaching sessions throughout the book. But it is also an investment model that finances itself; it generates enough income to cover its costs, so if you have to sit out some lean years, it won't cost you any money as long as you are managing your portfolio properly.

Leverage – the most important concept in property investing

Basically, leverage means using your money to get the best return – put simply, it's like paying someone a *little* bit of money to get you *more* money in return. And let's say you could invest £10,000 in two different ways, one growing to £11,000, the other growing to £20,000; which way would you choose? In property investment it is the leverage that makes it such a high performer. And key to this is the fact that for a small amount of your *own* money, you can end up controlling assets worth considerably more by using the bank's money. You're leveraging your small contribution to use the bank's money to make you a really good income.

Imagine you've inherited £100,000 – a nice proposition! Let's look at what you might do with it. One option is to use the lot to buy an investment property for cash, a house worth £100,000. Let's say that over ten years it's doubled in value and is now worth £200,000. During this time you've been taking home, say, £350 a month rental profit, a nice little extra income. Now, *another* option would be to use the £100,000 as *four* deposits on four properties, not just one, by using £300,000 of mortgage leverage to complete the purchase. Ten years later, your property is now worth 4 times £200,000, or £800,000. Now, look at how this is made up – your original £100,000 deposit, £300,000 of mortgage, and now £400,000 of profit, making your *total* equity £500,000. And it's that equity that you have earned, which you can use to extend your portfolio, or to pull down as cash – or both. Compare this with the first option where you invest the same amount but only generate £100,000 of profit.

Now, you might think there's just something wrong with having the £300,000 debt to the bank. Your instinct might say it's much better to buy the single house with cash and have no debt. But any really successful and wealthy business person lives with what to you or I might seem terrifying levels of debt. The difference is that it's what we call *good* debt, money that allows them to leverage their *own* money and make much more profit from it. Managed properly, it doesn't expose them or make them financially vulnerable, it simply makes their *own* money go much, much further in generating wealth. It's all to do with having an investor's 'mind-set', something I talk about in chapter 4.

'Controlling assets' – what does this mean?

One thing people sometimes get confused by is the idea of managing or *controlling* assets. It's easy to be mistaken and think that you can only make money from an asset if you actually own it. And this is wrong. With property investment, you only have a very small personal investment in the portfolio, typically just the deposit you pay to buy the first property. But you *control* the entire portfolio and, as such, it is *you* who draws back any or all of the profit as income. And this is why the most important concept in to understand in property investment is 'leverage' (see below). This is how you can invest a relatively modest sum and make it grow into million-pound-plus portfolios, the asset you control, without putting in any extra money.

Finally, I want to show you this simple investment model *(figure 6)*. Although simplified, it does demonstrate the basic principle of building a portfolio even if you ignore one of the most important rules, buying at discount (you will learn about this in chapter 5). I have been deliberately cautious in the model, using price increases of 5% a year and *not* factoring in compound increases. This means that over the full term of the model (20 years) you would expect even better results than these. When you reach chapter 9, we will have covered much more detail and you will see a more comprehensive model.

A simple example investment model

Year 1 You've saved your deposit of £25k and buy your first investment property. Its market value is £100k. You get a 75%LTV mortgage, using your £25k deposit for the remaining balance.	
Year 5 Value has increased each year and the property is now worth £130k. This means you can remortgage. The bank provides 75% of the new value (£97,500) giving you £22,500 cash to withdraw after repaying the original £75k mortgage. You use as a deposit for a second property.	
Year 10 Value for both properties has increased another 5% each year. Again you remortgage and release cash which you use as deposits on two new properties.	
Year 15 The same happens, and this time you buy four additional properties, giving you eight in all.	
Year 20 The same happens again, building your portfolio up to sixteen properties. And all you put in was the initial £25k on the first house! Imagine what little you would have earned in interest if you'd simply put that money into a high-interest savings scheme!	

figure 6

3. Meeting the coach

Steve felt uneasy. When he finally left Phil the other night, he'd gone home and talked non-stop for over an hour about Phil's coaching story. And Carol had quickly caught on to his enthusiasm. In fact it was she who had phoned the coach to make an appointment. But now as they sat in the slow-moving commuter traffic, Steve's mind was busy with printing schedules, machine maintenance and his delivery driver's request for paternity-leave. How could they possibly take on anything else just now, let alone becoming landlords to multiple tenants? Sensing his worry, Carol patted his knee reassuringly.

"Something on your mind, love?" she enquired.

"Half a dozen things, none of them good, and *none* of them to do with property or business coaching either. I don't know what we're doing … what *are* we doing?"

She laughed.

"All we're doing is checking it out, OK? Don't worry, the last thing I want is to take on another full-time job! But it could just be the answer to our financial future, and who knows, it may even mean we can cut down our hours before we're old and ready to drop … admit it, you're envious of Phil's lifestyle."

"Yeah, well – who wouldn't be?"

"There we are then – now stop worrying. If only this traffic would get moving; we're just a couple of streets away now."

Each fell into their own thoughtful silence as the cars trickled slowly forwards.

"Good afternoon! Or is it evening? Impossible to tell once the clocks have gone back!"

They were welcomed by a small, plump man in a striped suit with half-moon specs and a friendly twinkle in his eye. He reminded Carol of a distant cousin who had been an accountant – he certainly didn't look like a property tycoon. "So, you're friends of Phil I understand?"

"That's right. I'm Carol, and this is my husband, Steve."

They all shook hands and, following his gesture, sat in a pair of comfy seats in front of the desk. Carol thought it odd he hadn't introduced himself.

"Sorry – I didn't catch your name …"

"That's because I didn't give it." He chuckled. "Tell you what, just call me Coach, OK?"

Carol and Steve glanced at each other, wondering what they'd walked into. Seeing this, their host reassured them.

"It's what everyone calls me. So, let's get straight down to business."

Working regularly with couples, Coach had an intuitive ability to sense who was the chief motivator and who the reluctant support team. He could tell immediately that Carol was the one with the enthusiasm and focus, and so he invited her to outline their investment plan.

"Well, it was Steve's idea really," she glanced at her husband who was nervously inspecting his finger nails, "or his friend Phil's I suppose. Anyway, we talked it over non-stop last weekend and it makes so much sense. We're both experienced at running a business, and this is just the same, only renting out houses rather than printing, and—"

Coach put his hand up and interrupted her. "So you're thinking of taking on a second business?"

"No … well yes … well…" Carol felt cornered, realising Coach was far sharper than he looked. He smiled.

"Don't worry, it's part of my job to challenge, but I am on your side!" He looked at Steve as he said this, wanting the second part of his message to reassure him in particular. "I only asked that because we must be very clear from the start what you actually want to do here, what you plan to achieve."

"Oh well that's simple," Carol replied. "We want to make some serious money for the future so that we don't have to keep working stupid hours, so we can put the kids through college, so we can …" she added, glancing at Steve, "so we can take holidays together. You've no idea how much the business runs our lives at the moment."

Steve looked up and smiled, at last beginning to relax, sensing that Coach would somehow rein in Carol's enthusiasm and make sure they didn't do anything stupid. In response, Coach aimed his next question at Steve.

"So, this was originally your idea, but you're now having second thoughts; am I right?"

Steve uncrossed his legs. Now it was his turn to feel the laser-sharp focus of Coach's questions and it wasn't comfortable. He paused before replying, carefully composing his answer.

"Well … I think Carol's right, we need to generate more money somehow for the future; and people go on about work-life balance – ours is certainly out of kilter. But I just don't think we have the time, I mean it's easy shoving money off to a stockbrokers – they do all the work – but with this, we'd have to do everything. And there must be so much to learn and—"

Coach interrupted. "Now *that* is the one thing you've just said I would agree with … but we can come back to that. Carol, when you phoned you said you'd already done some research and found some properties?"

"Yes – in fact I've earmarked four and they're all—"

"Four? Goodness – you haven't wasted any time!" Was he being sarcastic? Steve frowned back while Carol shifted uneasily, sensing she was walking into another trap. But Coach smiled gently and invited her to tell him about the houses. Her enthusiasm quickly returned and to begin with, Coach just nodded silently.

"Well, the first one is two streets away from our house; I think it's a really good location, near the school. In fact they're all near schools – I remember how important that is from TV's Property Ladder. And it's on for £150,000 but I reckon we could get them down to £145,000; and three bedrooms, so the rent should be about £650–"

"OK, so far it sounds good – right number of bedrooms, location sounds about right and you're already talking discounted property which I like. But we'd need to examine these figures much more closely before making any decision—"

"Yes but—"

Coach held up his hand again. "Stick with the first house for a minute – what condition is it in?"

"Ah, well I've thought about that too, and priced the work. The kitchen's OK but I'd like to swap the black floor tiles for white ones – nice and bright; and there's this green carpet throughout the ground floor – it's not old but I think it looks a bit dated. Now, the living room is dark at one end, but I had a look at some of the neighbouring houses and we could do the same thing, knock through and put in a new window. Then there's the fire, one of those awful gas—"

Up went Coach's hand. Realising she had been gabbling, Carol felt a bit foolish.

"Steve – did you visit this house with Carol?" Steve nodded. "So what did *you* think about it?"

"I'm happy to leave all the decorating to my wife, same as at home!"

"Yes, but as an investment …?"

Steve was silent. Coach looked over to Carol who wasn't quite sure what to say. Coach left the silence hanging before pulling his chair closer to the desk and leaning forward towards them both. He looked serious.

"OK, first of all forget Property Ladder – that's just entertainment. Now, question one: what are you buying, a new home or a financial asset?" Carol opened her mouth to reply but Coach put his finger to his lips and continued.

"Question two: as well as looking in your own neighbourhood, did you compare the prices in different areas? And …" He paused to add drama to his last and most important question, "… who has helped you?"

Carol leaned forward and asked what he meant.

"Well, you've found some houses, you've decided you can get the price down, worked out the rent, costed the repairs and improvements – these are crucial figures, and decisions that will impact directly on the value of your investment. And to get these right you'll have needed some pretty good expert advice. So I'd be interested to see your financing and remortgaging projections for one of these houses.

Another heavy silence while Coach looked at them both over his glasses. Eventually he took them off and chuckled in the same warm way he had at the start of the session.

"Relax, both of you. I'm just playing 'bad cop', having a little fun." Neither Steve nor Carol seemed to appreciate this but he carried on. "We've only just met, and I need to learn a lot more about you, both individually and as a team; but listen, I do think you have exactly what it takes to become serious property investors." They both visibly relaxed. "But there's a lot to learn. And that's what I'm here for."

"So are you saying I've chosen the wrong houses then?" Carol needed some reassurance after his teasing.

"I couldn't possibly answer that without knowing a lot more. But I shouldn't have to answer it either. I'm not your advisor, I'm your coach; and my job is to teach *you* how to find the answer yourself. You could just as well ask if I agree about the colour of the carpet, but my personal opinion would be of no value. Neither in fact is yours because as I said, you are not buying a home, you're buying a *house*, an asset that will generate income. And, lesson one …" he paused to emphasise his conclusion, "… is to learn to *think like an investor*. And, if you want, I will help you."

He smiled and sat back again in his chair. Steve and Carol's faces showed that they were beginning to understand. Seeing this, Coach spoke again.

"Between you, you have the makings of a great partnership – you, Steve, are naturally cautious, and you don't want to be too distracted from your business, while Carol, you have energy *and* you're already thinking about location, schools and so on. This is good stuff. What we have to do is harness each of your strengths and then start developing a strategy – where you want to be, when, and how you'll get there."

By now they were really listening, their confidence in both the coach and themselves growing by the minute.

"But now, as all good therapists say, your time is up for today." He laughed at his little joke. "So I want you to do a little homework before we next meet."

Relieved to have something practical to do, Carol pulled her notebook from her bag and started to scribble in it.

"First – don't bother writing this bit Carol – yes I can help you learn all about property investing – or rather learn what it is you need to know. I call them the Core Competencies – everything from choosing the right house to knowing what to do about kitchen floor tiles! This will ensure you don't make the same expensive mistakes as many people. And you can then decide how much – or how little – you want to be directly involved in your property business."

Steve's face brightened when he heard this.

"But for now – and you can write this down if you like – I want you both to learn more about your own *attitudes* which may affect how you approach your investment project; and I want you to come back next time with the mind-set of *investors*. So, a little bit of soul-searching … you're successful business people so you've obviously done something right. But I bet you've made mistakes too? Taken bad advice? Or even not taken any advice at all? And don't just look at your business; think about how you are at home, as a family, as a couple. How do you spend money? Who makes the main decisions? How good are you at planning? And what happens when you don't stick to the plan or something unexpected happens?"

4. The mind-set of an investor

- **What's holding you back?**
- **The Home-owner's mind-set**
- **The Investor's mind-set**
- **Taking action!**

Q: *If property investment is such a great business prospect, and Steve and Carol are such good candidates, why was the coach so tough on them towards the end of their first session? Surely the job of a coach is to encourage not pour cold water on clients' enthusiasm?*

A: *The coach has in fact given them a strong head start, something that will help ensure they approach every aspect of their portfolio-building with the right mind-set.*

I can't stress enough that this book is about serious and successful long-term property investment. Yes, you can choose to be as hands-off as you want, but you will still be taking decisions that can make the difference between £30,000 a year income and nil income. And while this book aims to give you a lot of useful knowledge and information, without the right mind-set much of this will, quite frankly, be of little help. So in this chapter I'll help you to adopt an *investor's* mind-set. It's not scary, quite the opposite – the more you can think as an investor, the more excited you'll be about preparing your own portfolio. Like Carol and Steve you'll be chomping at the bit, and like them you'll have a strong head start.

So, this chapter is really important – and long! You may already be in the right mind-set but if not, take your time to read it, and come back to refresh your memory if you need to.

What's holding you back?

We all have different responses to something new or untested, and it's no different when faced with investment opportunities. But for anyone whose instinctive response is to back off, it's important to understand where that instinct comes from and be prepared to challenge it. With property investment, to generate the kinds of income I'm talking about we need to build portfolios worth impressive six or even seven figure sums, and that can seem very frightening. But once you understand this fear you can easily overcome it, especially when it's clear that it's not *your* fear anyway. So let's look more closely at what may be holding you back. Three things influence our readiness to invest – financial blueprint, earnings comfort zone, and FEAR. And there's one powerful external influence too – other people.

Financial blueprint

For most of us, this is the biggest obstacle to overcome, and one that could unravel your plans and stop you becoming a successful property investor. We all know how different influences help to shape us as children. But did you know that, by the age of 8-9, this includes our own *financial* blueprint, a set of beliefs about money, its value and how to spend it? It's true, and it can stick with us throughout life, influencing decisions, choices and even simple thoughts unless we recognise and challenge it. For example, there's nothing wrong in day-dreaming about having lots of money; we all do it from time to time. But many of us also feel there's something greedy or shameful about it – where does *that* come from?

The millionaire coach T. Harv Eker often refers to 'money blueprint' in his writing and his workshops, explaining it as the result of thoughts or ideas we have that come from parents, siblings, teachers and so on. And the ideas come in three ways – through the things we hear, like "money doesn't grow on trees!" and the things we see (for example, which parent managed the household money), and thirdly through specific experiences, anything from parents arguing over money to witnessing a robbery.

As adults, these become a kind of personal benchmark, a pre-set financial code of behaviour. Think of a thermostat, controlling the heating and air-conditioning in a room; opened windows or changing weather will affect the temperature briefly, but the thermostat will always return it to the pre-set level. It's the same with our money blueprint; you may have bold financial ambitions, but to achieve them you may have to examine – and *reset* – your own personal financial blueprint. T. Harv Eker talks about talented, successful people who never quite achieve all they could because of their money blueprint. They're not aware of this blueprint and even less that they can change it. But they can, and you can.

If you bear this in mind, you will see that when the opinions of Steve and Carol differ it's because they have slightly different money blueprints, and as well as learning how these might be holding them back, they also have to *understand each other's* if they are to work well together on their new enterprise. Fortunately they've got a good coach!

Earnings comfort zone

As wage-earning adults we tend to reinforce our money blueprint with our expectations about earnings. It's typical to see someone aged 25, earning say £30,000 a year, who ten years later, factoring in inflation and modest incremental rise, is still earning effectively the same. This income has become embedded in their mind as what they expect. So if circumstances change and their income drops they will probably look for ways to top it back up to £30,000, this being their personal financial comfort zone. The problem with this, added to our inherited attitudes to money, is that it makes it very hard to imagine anything different. And so, when offered an investment opportunity, many people find it really hard to consider it even if they can see it is minimal risk. As long as they are hanging on to the £30,000, life's good.

Fear

It's time we introduced an acronym! So here's one, FEAR – False Expectation Appearing Real. And it's a really useful one too. The key word in FEAR is 'False', because to overcome FEAR we must challenge false beliefs. In fact, overcoming FEAR will help you to take your first big step *as soon as possible* which, as I explain at the end of this chapter, is really important to your future success as a property investor.

Being cautious is natural and can be a life-saver in all kinds of situations, but we need to decide if our fear is realistic or false. Think of the person who is scared of heights and won't go up the Eiffel Tower, convinced they will fall off. We can all find examples like this in our own ways of behaving – things driven by an embedded misbelief. And wherever this misbelief comes from – our parents, friends or just our own imagination

– we need to recognise and challenge it. So, if you find yourself hesitating at any stage when reading this book, ask yourself what scares you and whether it's a real fear or a false expectation of imminent disaster!

Blame someone else!

The three forces I've just described all play games inside our own minds, but there is a simpler *external* influence on our choices – other people. Rob Moore, one of the UK's great speakers on property investment, talks about *sheep and crabs*[3] as an analogy for what stops people investing in property. He explains how other people might be holding us back, and how to recognise the individuals who will actually help us succeed.

Sheep are people who follow the crowd or copy their friends, sticking closely to what is familiar rather than making their own analysis of what is good or bad. They are not out to 'get you' but they can be a bad influence. Regarding property investment, sheep follow their own kind rather than looking independently for expert help. So they might buy the same type of investment flat as their friend, make the same mistakes and have the same bad experience. Or of course they follow the crowd by avoiding property altogether. Either way, while sheep are harmless in themselves, as a flock they are very powerful and it can be hard to resist being drawn in.

Crabs, on the other hand, will deliberately hold you back and try to stop you doing what you want. Rob Moore calls them crabs for a very good reason. Fishermen's crab pots don't have lids because they don't need them – if one crab tries to crawl

....

3 Make Cash in a Property Market Crash (Rob Moore & Mark Homer, 2008)

out of the top, the others in the pot will reach up and pull it back down. So if you're trying to start out and build your investment portfolio, the crabs are the people who will do everything they can to talk you out of it. And once you've learned how to identify crabs and sheep, you don't have to dump them as friends! Just understand why their attitudes are not helpful.

So ...

... by reading this book you're already well on the way to overcoming any or all of the things that otherwise might hold you back. But you *will* hesitate, you *will* have moments when FEAR kicks in, and there will always be people who criticise; but remember, this doesn't mean you are striking out alone. There are many people and investment organisations ready to support you. And as our couple's next coaching session reveals, get the right expert team around you and you'll soon wonder why you ever let anything hold you back!

The Home-owner's mind-set

Now, remember Carol in the first coaching session, and the house she described? You wouldn't believe how often I've heard this from new clients. And it is perfectly understandable, the kind of mind-set you can expect from anyone like you or me whose own home has been a huge focus of money, time and investment. But it's no good if you want to be a serious property investor, building a sizeable portfolio of highly profitable properties. You're not dabbling, you're looking at bringing in a six-figure lump sum or a five-figure annual income. And like Steve and Carol, your retirement or your children's university fees could be at stake!

So, to dump the home-owner mind-set we need to work from a different perspective. I'm not advocating the rogue landlord who expects tenants to live in slum conditions! It's just a case of being more practical and realistic than we might be with our own homes. If the kitchen tiles are in good condition and safe, then the colour is not important. If the carpet has several years' good life left in it, why change it? It is the location, the number of rooms and the condition, not the style, that will make it rent. So, think *practical*.

Here's an example based on true figures. Let's say you live in a £250,000 house. You've looked around for something similar because this is the market sector you're most familiar with, and you've found a house in your area for a bargain sale price of £150,000. It will rent for £600pcm which seems OK. But in a neighbouring district there's a house with an asking price of £88,000. We also establish we can buy it for a discount, for £75,000, and it will rent for £560pcm. The maths is easy; instead of your home-from-home, you could have bought *two* houses for the same money and brought in nearly double the rent.

I'm based in North Yorkshire where I know I could find, for the same price, one property in York or two in, say, Scarborough, all with equally strong rental demands. I know you will find similar illustrations wherever you are in the country. Remember though that buying for less does not have to mean sacrificing quality. You're not trying to find run-down wrecks just to get a cheap bargain – you're buying a business asset, and the more you have to spend on maintenance, the more you risk renting at a deficit.

Many of my own clients began by putting some spare cash into one house, then another, but without knowing much about it all. By getting expert help they were able to turn this around, but think of the years of profitable investment they wasted! And one last point – you don't have to keep your investment house(s) for evermore either. We'll talk later in the book about what to do if a property's performance deteriorates, but for now just be reassured that unlike your own home, you can – and must – make tough, dispassionate decisions about your portfolio.

The Investor's mind-set

I hope by now my key message is coming through clearly – building a profitable property portfolio with good income potential is a serious business. However, it needn't be time-consuming! There are plenty of experts able to manage all aspects of the operation if you wish. But what you *will* have to do yourself is to define your goals. And remember, property investing is not sexy, it isn't about getting rich quick; to achieve reliable and sizeable returns we're looking at a ten-year plan at the very least – unless of course you're flipping, buying a property to renovate and then resell, which is something we touch on in chapter 16.

So you do need to take some positive action soon, and this starts with adopting the investor's mind-set with specific regard to:

- **Goals and plans**
- **Risk and loss**
- **Profit and market trends**
- **Good and bad debt**

Goals and plans

Remember when you first started out in business or started on your career ladder? Back then you had vision – OK, with loads of energy, time, enthusiasm and so on – but above all a vision of what you wanted to achieve. And it's exactly what you need now, a vision to shape your portfolio. As an investor you'll need to define some goals and then plan how to reach them.

I like to compare this to an athlete preparing for the Olympics. Because she's aiming for gold in the marathon, she's hardly going to settle for a 3-mile run once a week over the next four years. She knows that she's going to need strength, stamina and even pain management skills. And acquiring these involves many considerations – diet, rest, exercise, medical care, recovery from injury, and so on. In other words, the goal may seem simple – coming first in a long race – but the planning is anything but simple.

How does this compare with property? Well, your goal might be to generate an income of £30,000 a year for the rest of your life. It won't happen overnight, and it won't happen unless you buy the right properties. It also won't happen unless you manage each property's income generation well *and* monitor their market value within a fluctuating economy. Take a look at this: say you buy a house for £100,000. After ten years, the *increase* in its value could vary as much as £30,000-£50,000 depending on what you buy. So everything you do from selecting and buying to retaining or selling off will affect your total achievement by the end of this period.

The next coaching session explains in detail all the different tasks and decision that will affect the return on your investment. For now, another acronym, and one I'm sure you are familiar with – SMART. It describes how to ensure your goals are Specific, Measurable, Attainable, Realistic and Timely:

- **S**pecific: you need clear answers to *who, what, where, when, which and why?*
- **M**easurable: and to *how much? How many? How will I know?*
- **A**ttainable: for which you need the right attitude, skills and financial capacity
- **R**ealistic: a goal you are both *willing* and *able* to work for
- **T**imely: contained within a defined time-frame.

All of these apply to property investing and illustrate the role of good planning. And it is so important to have a goal that I want you to pause for a moment and think about your own. Think about personal as well as financial goals as they often overlap, and note them down in this space below. It will be a useful reminder for when you dip back into the book in the future and firm up your plans:

....

....

....

....

....

....

....

....

Of course planning is not just about setting your goals and managing your money safely, it also covers cushioning yourself against things going wrong – understanding the level of risk and the potential for loss ...

Risk and loss

... and you do this by keeping the right balance between cash flow, savings and investments. There is risk in property investment just as there is in any financial investment. Your aim is to understand and manage this risk.

Anthony Robbins, a successful Business, Life and Personal Coach, has a very good way of looking at it all. He talks about 'buckets of money' – *security bucket, investment bucket and dream bucket.* Your *security bucket* holds the money you make sure is always there – cash, savings, premium bonds etc – money you can easily get to and which is always safe. Your *investment bucket* holds the money you *could* afford to lose if you had to, for example stocks and shares, or even a 'buy and hold' property which you buy and hang onto. And your *dream bucket* contains a little money put aside for the things you dream about – a yacht, early retirement, a trip round the world. As you go through life, the balance between your buckets will change. For example, when you're young you can afford to put more into your investment bucket because if things go wrong there's still time to start again. But as you get older you tend to redirect some money away from investment and into the security bucket. With less time to put things 'right' we need to go for what feels the safest option.

However, if you understand that the risk is *not* as great as you thought, you can have more confidence to allocate your money as you wish. And that is what this entire book is all about – earning your *financial freedom*. Some people regard any investment as a gamble, simply because the outcome cannot be guaranteed. But gambling is based mostly on luck or chance. By contrast, property investment is one of the least chance-driven investments you can make. You can read more about the potential downsides in chapter 15, but the key to getting it right is to know what you're doing – so read this book, follow the advice and you will become an expert and have the confidence to make a success of it.

Profit and market trends

Let's assume you've silenced your home-owner's instinct and are now rating potential properties as business assets. This means you'll be thinking about how these assets will perform. So, remember the statistics in chapter 2. This is not a fast-buck scheme but a solid investment model based on long term trends. And if you manage your money buckets well, you will always be cushioned against small, short-term downturns. So, as the size of your future income or lump-sum depends on the value increase of your portfolio, your mind-set needs to be a long term one that doesn't panic at the first dip in values.

You also need to study and know the *current* market each time you buy a property. As our couple will learn shortly, the coach will expect them to buy houses at a *discount*. It's perfectly possible, so why lose future profit by paying the asking price?

Good and bad debt

Many of my clients struggle at first to grasp the concept of *good debt,* and it's not their fault. Thinking about investments shows you take your finances seriously, in which case you probably view debt as an irritating fact of life, the first thing you'd wipe out if you won the lottery. If so, I'm going to make your day! Debt is *good*. No, not all debt, but the type that lets you build a personal fortune and brings you financial security.

In essence, any debt will bring with it an additional cost, typically an interest charge. The difference between good and bad debts comes down to what you get out of the debt. A good debt generates more return than it costs to maintain. In other words, financially it makes a profit. So, with our property investment strategy, your mortgage will generate tax-efficient revenue greater than the borrowing costs of the mortgage itself.

Another way to think about it is in terms of your assets. Take your own house and your car; you may regard these as assets but they also generate expenses – electricity bills, MOT and servicing, etc. – which have to be met with money from a different source. The mortgages supporting your portfolio are debts, but with the repayments covered by the rental income you don't have to earn any extra money to service them. And as illustrated at the end of chapter 2, you can then generate a realistic annual income from your portfolio within, typically, ten years.

So, a real investor's asset is one that makes money whether or not you get out of bed, whether you're in the office or lying on the beach. And this can include a good debt. I can really recommend you read Robert Kiyosaki's book "Rich Dad, Poor Dad"[4] which explains good and bad debt in ways we can all relate to.

....

4 Published London, Time Warner 2002

Taking action!

OK, so now you have a good overview of the investor's mind-set. You might have had this already but if not, you can be contemplating it as you work through the rest of the book. You'll also understand that property investment is long term investment, looking to the future. So what better reason for getting started NOW? Exactly how to do this is covered in chapter 17, but for now, as the most common hurdle is 'fear of getting it wrong', I'll leave you with this to think about:

Successful people make far more mistakes than other people for two reasons: 1) they are more willing to step forward, try something and risk it going wrong – but at least they try, and 2) if 8 out of 10 times they get it right, multiply that up, comparing to someone who doesn't take any steps at all through fear of getting it wrong, and you can see why ultimately they are the successful people!

5. The key rules in property investing

"Well, you've both done excellent homework, I'm delighted!" Coach clapped his hands and beamed at them.

Steve and Carol had spent the first five minutes of the session convincing Coach that they now understood what he'd said the last time and were clear about their objectives – they wanted to learn how to invest properly, avoid mistakes and build up a profitable portfolio. Coach was relieved as, without this change in mind-set, they wouldn't have been able to move on to the more exciting topics. He'd had one client who'd never got beyond this stage and in the end had to give up any idea of property investment. Fortunately Steve and Carol were approaching it as a business, and even if they decided to hire experts or have the properties managed for them, they wanted to know exactly what was happening and why.

"So, today we start looking at the core competencies, the things a successful property investor needs to know and understand. And where better to start than with the rules?"

Steve and Carol looked at each other with a mix of anticipation and nervousness. They were still a little wary of Coach but were eager to learn. Carol was once again the scribe, bringing out a brand new ring binder with a crisp new pad of paper attached. Steve just clutched his pocket calculator.

"Carol, that folder will be very useful. I'll be giving you both some hand-outs today, and you wouldn't believe the number of times I've seen clients stuff them into pockets or bags. I can see you'll be much more organised than that!"

Steve sniggered at this but Coach ignored him.

"So – the rules. I'm starting with these because they will become the foundation of everything else you learn with me.

And they exist for a very good reason – to stop you making mistakes."

"You mean like not replacing perfectly good green carpet, that kind of thing?" Steve asked.

"Oh no, something far more important than that," Coach replied.

Carol resisted giving Steve her 'told you so' look and they both waited for Coach to explain.

"These rules make sure you buy the *right* property and buy it for the right *price.*"

Opening a file on the desk in front of him, Coach took out two pieces of paper *(figure 7)* and handed them across to Steve and Carol. He gave them a moment to read in silence:

Hand-out 1

	The Rules
1	Buy at the right price, always with discount
2	Buy the right type of property
3	Only buy with the right cash flow
4	Check rental demand before purchase
5	Have a rental contingency fund
6	Put as little money as possible in each house

figure 7

"Wow," said Steve thoughtfully, "I guess this is why it's best to work with a coach, to get this type of inside information."

"Ah no," Coach corrected him, "these aren't just *my* rules."
Steve looked up puzzled.

"This is the distillation of what I learned by interviewing over twenty different landlords, each with over a hundred properties. These rules are thoroughly road-tested!"

"Bear in mind," Coach added, "that these are the rules for *buy to let* investment – so they concern the type of houses we're interested in, 3-4 beds, town centre, ex-council or terraced. If you wanted to buy property to do up and sell, or go into HMOs[5] for that matter, you'd need a completely different set of rules. I can teach you those too some other time, but just remember, *these* are the rules that will help you become buy to let investment experts."

Steve and Carol both nodded seriously.

"OK, let's work through them. **Rule one – 'buy at the right price, *always* with discount'**. What do I mean here?"

Steve shrugged his shoulders, not sure what to say.

"Buy at a discount?" Carol suggested.

"Exactly," Coach replied. "I'll talk more about this in a moment, but for now just realise that you can easily knock down asking prices of some houses by at least 15%. So with a sizeable discount, you've effectively made instant profit! And I mean 15%; don't go for one only offering 10%!"

Carol raised her hand. "Surely we're just talking small margins here? There must be some times when it's still a good house even at 10% discount?"

"Absolutely not!" Coach replied forcefully, causing them both to jump. "It's a rule remember, and it's there for a reason! Some people easily get up to 25% discount. As a serious investor, you will never ever buy at less than 15%."

....

5 House of Multiple Occupancy

They both nodded meekly.

"Your discount, you see, is your immediate profit, but it stays in the house until you release money in the future through refinancing. So, it's all about hunting down the property with the best discount – more of that later."

He paused for moment to let Carol finish writing her notes.

"Ok. **Rule two – 'buy the right type of property'.** Any ideas?"

Steve decided to wait and hear what Coach had to say. Carol blushed, remembering the last session and her over-enthusiastic description of the house she'd found. Coach noticed.

"I think *you* know, don't you Carol?" She nodded and he continued. "In essence, buy the houses that have the most *investment value*. Forget homes, remember, think investment."

Steve felt Carol was being got at a little and tried to defend her.

"But Carol's house was a great house – you said yourself it had a good location, schools and so on, and she said she could get a discount too."

"Sure thing," Coach agreed, "but it's still not giving the best performance, not for a serious investor. It comes down to maths. You buy a house for £150,000 and rent it out for £650 a month – *or* for the same money, somewhere else, you buy two houses, each at £75,000 and renting at, say, £560 a month – what's the difference?"

Again Steve was punching numbers and excitedly answered Coach.

"Well, nearly double the rent for a start!"

"Exactly. And although we're in this for long term asset growth, a little bit of extra income can be very useful for meeting unexpected costs – or just for giving yourselves a treat!" He smiled at them.

It was time for **Rule three – 'only buy with the right cash flow'.** This was right in Steve's comfort zone and he settled in his chair, calculator at the ready.

"OK, cash flow. It's a business with regular income and expenditure. But we need it to be *cash flow positive*, which means you never have to put in any of your own money. Income always exceeds expenditure. And the rule is never to buy a house that will be cash flow positive by less than £50 a month – and that's after expenses which could include the letting agent's fee if you use one. Add it up over a year and it's not much, but it's enough to feed into your contingency fund and cover any empty periods between tenants. So, *always* working from conservative estimates " he paused, looking over his glasses as he always did to emphasise a point, "let's add up those outgoings, and we'll work on my £75,000 example."

They made a comical pair, Carol with her pen poised over her pad, Steve with his finger hovering above the calculator, but Coach was delighted with his eager students.

"Steve – do you want to punch in some figures? OK, first we have the rent coming in, lets' say £560. Now, let's assume a mortgage at 6%, as it would be if the economy was in better shape – so that's a monthly £290 or so; add in maintenance costs of £80, about average for this type of property; finally letting agent fees, usually 10% of the rent, and buildings insurance at, say, £15 – and what do we get?"

"£441," they both replied in unison.

"So, with our rent at £560, minus £441, we've made £119, well over our £50 target. And of course, as the interest rate is actually lower at the moment, we can put aside a little more each month for the time being. Now Carol, did you get all that?"

She nodded, showing him her neat notes *(figure 8)*.

Rental income:	£560
Less outgoings	
Mortgage (6%)	(£290)
Maintenance	(£80)
Letting agent	(£56)
Insurance	(£15)
Total outgoings	(£441)
Cash flow (must be greater than £50)	£119

figure 8

Coach was about to continue when Steve raised a question.

"OK, so we're cash flow positive, but we're never going to be able to retire on £50 a month! We'd have to buy , I don't know – thirty houses?"

"Steve, you don't understand," Coach replied patiently, "we're talking about the working cash flow, not your investment income. Your early retirement is funded by the growth in the property values and your asset accumulation. This positive cash flow is simply to ensure you never have to put in any of your own money to top up running costs."

"I see!" Steve was clearly relieved.

Nodding approvingly, Coach continued.

"Remember, these are rules based on the experience of many, many people over a very long time, and they work. For example," off came the glasses, "you find a house offering an irresistible £30,000 discount, but if it's going to be even just £1 negative in cash flow, you should *not* buy it. Otherwise the benefits of the longer term investment are reduced each and every time you end up dipping into your own personal funds to keep the thing afloat."

Looking serious, they both nodded their agreement. They were beginning to see that these rules really made a lot of sense.

Coach then launched into **Rule four – 'check rental demand before purchase'.**

"It's not enough to buy a house in an area that generally rents well, you need to have good evidence that you'll get tenants queuing up, not just when you first rent it but every time tenants leave too."

"That's exactly what Phil said!" exclaimed Steve.

"Well, he learned from the best…" Coach laughed. "Anyway, it's simple. Say you bid on a house and your offer is accepted. You're not committed to the purchase yet, OK? So in the five or six weeks it takes to complete the deal, advertise it, take out an—"

"But surely that's risky?" Carol interrupted. "What if we don't get the house?"

"There's no problem – you haven't yet actually offered it to anyone have you?"

Carol shrugged in agreement.

"Look," Coach continued, "all I'm talking about is this." And he showed them an advertisement torn out from a newspaper *(figure 9)*.

Houses/rooms to let section

3-bed semi, Every St, Somewhere. DG, GCH, £125/wk, bonds & refs required. Tel Steph on 01234 567890

figure 9

"But what you *are* doing, before signing on the dotted line, is making sure you'll get tenants. And the golden rule is – any fewer than ten applicants and you don't buy the house. You're testing the water and it's very important to do it."

"Just like product-testing then?" Steve asked and then turned to Carol. "You remember that new print finish we nearly invested in? The one we tested over the Christmas period? We'd have lost thousands if we'd bought the wretched machine." Turning to Coach he explained. "We did all the right things – hyping up the new service, generating interest with special offers – you name it, we did it – and still got very little response. Although we'd believed the salesman, thank goodness we insisted on a no-obligation trial."

"There you are then. And with this it's much easier too; it only costs about £25 to run an advert – just name the street, quote the number of rooms, mention bond and references and give a phone number.

"Now – we're over half way through the rules – do you want a quick break?" he asked, but they both shook their heads, keen to hear what was still to come.

"OK then – where were we – oh yes, **Rule five – 'have a rental contingency fund'.** Again, it's a really obvious rule but one that some people still ignore. Now, I'm assuming you'd never try to run your business without money for emergencies? Of course not. And it's just the same with your portfolio. And," he chuckled and smiled kindly at Carol, "this is the one time it *does* pay to think like a home-owner! The boiler breaks down, the bathroom floods, roof tiles blow off in a gale, the fence collapses onto the neighbours car … all of these can, and probably will, happen, so you must always have money put aside to cover them. £3,000 is usually enough for a portfolio of five properties, and you need it from the start. But of course any rental profit can be added – and remember to keep it in the same separate account you use for collecting rent. It's just another way you keep the business and your personal finances safely separate."

"And finally, my favourite rule, **Rule six – 'put as little money as possible into each house'.** Why is it my favourite? Because it reflects the beauty of the entire property investment model, one which makes the best use of someone else's funding to generate your own profit."

"You make it sound really dodgy!" Steve said.

"Not at all. Buy to let mortgages are there for exactly this purpose, to allow people like you and me to build portfolios without having to rely on personal money. As expert property investors, you'll know which financial advisor to turn to for help, one who understands your need to spread your money across a growing portfolio, not just one house."

Carol stopped writing and looked up.

"I think I understand. The more properties we have in the portfolio, the more asset growth we get."

"Exactly!" Coach replied. "So, with a £60,000 deposit you should work the mortgages in such a way that you can get two properties to start with. And then having bought at the minimum 15% discount, in six months you'll be able to remortgage and release enough of your original deposits to buy *another* property. Three properties from the original £60,000!"

Steve was now looking very impressed, reassured that there was nothing remotely 'dodgy' about it. He started to ask a question but Coach rose slowly from his chair. "Good time for a break I think – I certainly need to stretch my legs. We'll come back another time to look in detail at the financing but for now why not take another look through the list of rules and I'll sort out some coffee?"

6. Investing in the right property

- **Finding the right property**
- **The motivated seller**
- **Employing the experts**
- **Valuing a property**

Finding the right property

"Time flies! We're over half way through today's session – so we'd better push on."

"Just before we do, can I ask a question?" Carol spoke up. "I can see my four houses weren't great choices, but I knew the area – they were easy to find. How are we supposed to know where to find the right properties? Neither of us have time to drive around for hours on end."

"Well, I'll let you into a secret ..." They both leaned forward. "My team, when sourcing properties for clients, find out almost everything without leaving their desks. Of course, doing this day in, day out, they know exactly what they're looking for. But so will you in time. You need to find out about the neighbourhood, the history of recent sale prices *plus* details of other properties for sale in the area, and then of course the likely rental income. Then, with all of this, you just need to speak to your experts and do the sums."

"So, presumably we still have to look for ones that are actually for sale?" Steve was a bit confused. "How can we do that from behind a desk?"

"Use the internet!" Coach explained. "Almost all of your due diligence work can be done online."[6]

"You mean property-for-sale websites, ones like Rightmove?" Carol asked.

"Yes, although you won't necessarily find all the sellers on the websites, not the sellers that *we* are interested in. I'll explain in a moment. But you will be able to check out the type of houses, the neighbouring streets, local amenities, schools and so on – it all gives you a good profile of the area. And for the rent question, if you work on the premise that you can charge £20 a month more than LHA – sorry, that's Local Housing Allowance – then again, a quick internet search should give you some reliable figures."

Steve chipped in. "You also said we had to speak to experts?"

"Well, all this gives you a really good understanding of the area, the house and its potential income, but you still need to check with your finance or mortgage advisor that you can get the right deal, and of course you're looking for a discount remember. It's also sensible to check with your tradespeople about any repairs needed and likely maintenance costs."

Steve nodded, feeling increasingly relieved that there were experts to help them. Carol however was frowning and asked the next question.

"This all makes great sense, but this discount thing still confuses me – how do we *know* if we're getting the right discount? I mean, how do we know if the sale price is an accurate market value? Don't sellers expect buyers to haggle a bit? Won't they push their asking price up to account for this?"

....

6   You can find a list of websites in chapter 20: Useful resources.

Coach pushed his chair back, smiling. "A very good question to ask, and one that shows you are now approaching this as an investor! The answer really lies in becoming an expert in house values and in knowing the market. It's one of the ways in which it can really pay to get expert help. But I can give you a guideline. Look on the Rightmove website, and properties there generally sell for 93%[7] of the final price advertised. So, if you chip away and get a £100,000 house for £95,000 you've probably still paid over the odds. Now, I mentioned earlier that you should always aim for around 15% discount, yes?"

Carol nodded while Steve reached for his calculator.

"Well, that's 15% off its true value. So, if you know your £100,000 house should really sell on the open market for £93,000 – start with *that* figure and then factor in your target 15% discount, meaning you pay no more than—"

"£79,050!" Steve looked up triumphantly.

"Exactly. So you're right to ask about values, and I'll mention this again right at the end. But for now just remember that knowing how it all works in theory is *not* the same as having up to date market expertise. If it did, experts like me would be out of a job!"

The motivated seller

"But do people really drop their prices that much?" Carol asked, looking puzzled.

"Oh yes," Coach replied, "people do – and not just the poor unfortunates who've lost their job or gone bankrupt. There can be other reasons too. Usually the key thing is that, for

....

7   Based on a survey conducted by Rightmove in 2011.

the owner, selling fast is more important than price. Take a look at this." And he handed them another sheet of paper, this one headed 'Motivated Sellers' *(figure 10)*. They read down through the long list.

Hand-out 2	
Motivated sellers – why they need a quick sale	
Reason	*Some common causes*
Need to relocate	Emigrating Better school for the children New job To be closer to older relatives Moving to a nursing home
Change in household size or needs	Children now at college, fees need paying Retirement Death of spouse or partner Divorce Redundancy
Financial	Facing repossession Bankruptcy To raise money for a project (e.g. business investment) Broken chain (house buying) Probate (deceased person's estate needs to sell)
Investors	Tired landlords (taken on too much) Need money for another investment
Other	Owner in prison Bad experiences in the house Area/neighbourhood has changed Local development planned

figure 10

"That's amazing!" Steve said, "I'd never have thought of some of these, but looking at them it's kind of obvious."

"Quite. What they all have in common is *a need to sell quickly*; price alone is not their prime driver. But, as I mentioned earlier, they may not appear on websites – they may not even have the house up for sale yet."

"Really?" Carol asked. "So how are we supposed to find them?"

Coach paused and looked through his papers on the desk trying to find the schedule of coaching topics. "Oh dear, I really must be more organised. Anyway, if I remember rightly, it's in the next session that we talk about finding motivated sellers. But what's useful for now is to think about the psychology of it all."

Steve gave Coach a curious look.

"What I mean is this; we're talking about people who might be under tremendous pressure, emotional as well as financial."

"I can believe that," Carol replied, tapping her list. "Some of these reasons could be a bit embarrassing for the seller. If it was me in these situations, I'm not sure I'd want to talk about it to a complete stranger."

Coach nodded in agreement. "That's why building up trust is so important – *and* being completely honest yourself. Remember, you are not trying to swindle anyone out of their money; you're simply looking for good value purchases, which can mean helping someone out of a tricky corner at the same time. But it's useful to be able to anticipate the amount of stress the property might be causing the seller."

Coach saw that Steve was deep in thought, still studying the list.

"Steve, which sellers from the list are likely to be the least stressed?"

Steve ran his finger down the list before replying.

"I guess – well, relocation's one? I mean, maybe the seller's got a promotion or a new job, and the family is stuck in the old house until they sell."

Coach laughed. "Spot on, and the entire family will thank you! But if you think about it, that's about the only one not tinged with some kind of sad event or bad news." They both nodded agreement. "So you see, it's vital that you approach people in a simple and up-front professional manner. It makes it easier for them to discuss matters – *and* for you to spot the ones who are likely to pull out at the last minute. Believe me, some investors waste huge amounts of time chasing motivated sellers who turn out not to be all that motivated after all."

Employing the experts

"Goodness," he said suddenly, glancing at the clock on the wall behind them, "time's almost up – and I've got two more things to cover. The first is just to touch on expert help. I just want to make sure you understand what's available. Different people go for different levels of help, and with what you're learning, you'll be more than capable of deciding *when* to use it!

"I do recommend however that when you're just starting out, as *you* are, finding the right properties at the right price is much easier if you use an expert to source the property. Especially if you don't want to devote hours and hours and drive yourselves mad trying to compare this one with that. A good company will be constantly looking for investment properties and motivated sellers, so they'll already have a long list of them before you've even logged onto the internet! They'll also have checked the rental income potential, and will know the discount you should be able to command."

"I must say, it sounds sensible … I just don't know …" Carol hesitated.

"There's no decision to make here and now," Coach reassured her. "And no pressure – it's just a hassle-free way of getting your properties. You still need to know how to check a deal thoroughly so that when an expert puts it your way you can assess it and make the right decision. And I think," he checked his watch, "yes, we've just got time to look at that now, how to value a property."

Valuing a property

"Right," Coach suggested, "I think it'll be much easier to talk you through this using the internet. Why don't you both come round this side of the desk so you can see over my shoulder?"

As the desk was almost against the window there wasn't much space, and although they both managed to squeeze in, they didn't look at all comfortable. Coach had another idea.

"Tell you what, one of you sit in my chair and operate the internet – I'll stand here and guide you through it."

Steve looked eagerly at Carol who grinned back, seeing the little boy within who wanted to press the buttons. He promptly sat down in Coach's chair and waited for instructions.

"Right … the key thing here is to save yourself a huge amount of time and, obviously, to avoid buying the wrong house. OK, there are four websites I use regularly, and you're going to want to jump between them easily so make sure you open up a new window for each site. Now, let's imagine you've heard of a house for sale; seems to be a good area, fair price and so on. What we're trying to do here is find out what it's *really* worth today, right now. So, the first thing is to visit the house and find out what other houses nearby have been selling for."

They both looked up at him surprised. He laughed.

"Not literally, no – using the internet. Steve, click on the Google Earth icon would you?"

Steve did this and the site opened.

"Good. I should point out that if you haven't used Google Earth before you'll be asked to download it, but that's easy to do. Now, using Google Earth we can see recent photos of the street and, hopefully, the property itself. Type in – oh, why not type in your own address?"

Steve did this.

"Wow – look Carol, there's our street! You can even see that old camper van that never moves!"

"Ah, you can do better than that – use those cursors," he pointed at the screen, "and you should be able to get down to street level – yes, there you are, and now you can pan the camera up and down the street until you find your house."

Steve had a quick play.

"OK, what we need to do is find out whether all the houses are pretty much the same or all different. We want to get a feel for prices in the street. And," he peered down at the screen, "I think they're all quite similar."

Carol and Steve's street was made up of terraced houses, all built at roughly the same time.

"You see," Coach continued, "this isn't an *exact* science, just a guide to values, but had all the houses been different styles and sizes we wouldn't have been able to get reliable information this way. So this is good. Now, let's see how typical your street is of the neighbourhood by checking out some nearby streets – if you don't know the names, just type in the first part of your postcode and it'll go back to aerial view – then you can select a local street. This just gives you more of an idea, useful if it's an area you're not familiar with."

"Right, so we know what the house and nearby houses look like; time to open a new window and type in www.rightmove. co.uk. This is where we start valuing the house. Got it open? Good, can you type in the postcode please – if it comes with no results, try within a quarter of a mile of the postcode. OK, now you see it's asking you to specify what you're looking for – let's go for 3-4 bedrooms."

"Wow," Carol said, "there are a lot of houses for sale!"

"Yes, but we're only interested in a few," Coach explained. "We might have a list of only half a dozen, or as many as 30; the point is we want to look at the 4th and 5th cheapest of these to get our average price. Then, remember, most houses sell for around 7% less than the asking price so we also deduct 7% from the 4th and 5th cheapest."

Steve looked up, a little confused.

"What I mean is, with this method you can tell whether the one you've got your eye on is over-priced or not. If it's more expensive than the 4th or 5th cheapest it's probably not a good option and there'll be others that will be cheaper and provide better discounts too."

"OK, I've got that," Steve replied, "so what's the third website?"

"Slow down," Coached laughed, "while you've got Rightmove open it's a good idea to check the nearby streets as well, especially if you feel that your target house is a wee bit expensive. So you just do the same but extend the radius of the Rightmove search. But yes, let's push on for now and pull up the third site – can you type in www.nethouseprices.com – this is just another way to check the value, this time based on the history of house sales in the area. OK, once again, put in the postcode and …"

He waited while Steve typed it all in.

"There, what we can see is a history of house sales over the past ten years. And if you want, you can pop back over to Google Earth and see the actual house as well. Right, the last website – new window remember – is www.nationwide.co.uk/hpi.

"Now, this is an index of house prices run by the Nationwide Building Society. See there, you can type in different dates. So we type in the sale price when our target house was last sold, and then it will work out what its approximate sale price today should be. And what I would do is check this for the last ten houses sold in the street – remember, you can get them from nethouseprices.com – and ignore the ones at both extremes; some might have had a conservatory added or be in a really bad state of repair. We want a good reliable average, so it's best to look at the middle six or seven ones from the list."

"I must say," Carol interrupted, "it seems a fiddly business, even if we can do it from the comfort of an armchair."

"I know," Coach smiled, "and I reckon just to buy one single property we can look at a good 60 properties, all obtainable for at least 25% below genuine market value! But believe me, with practice you get really quick at this and it's your financial future at stake – it pays to look for the very best deals. You can actually pay a company called Home Track to do it for you – it costs about £20 for a report – but it's a really good idea to do this internet research yourself as well. As an investor, you're developing a nose for property so the more practice you get, the better.

"Now, very last question for today; we've learned how to value a property, but there's one other thing we need to value. Any ideas?"

They were both so tired from concentrating on the internet that neither offered an answer.

"The rent!" Coach declared. "Buying at the right price is one thing, but you also need to know it will bring in enough rent to be cash flow positive. And an easy way to do this, again using the internet, is to look up Local Housing Authority (LHA) rents – https://lha-direct.voa.gov.uk/search.aspx – and assume that you can get the LHA amount plus, say, twenty pounds a month."

He looked down at them both huddled in front of the computer.

"And that's it for today! Lots to think about, and particularly to try out at home on the internet."

7. Negotiating on your purchases

- **The emotions of the negotiation**
- **Looking for motivated sellers**
- **Closing the deal**

Steve and Carol had discussed their previous session at length, both struck by how much work it all seemed to involve. Carol had started to talk about stepping back and paying people to manage it all for them, but Steve reminded her that they had always been the kind of people who wanted to accomplish things for themselves. He pointed out that this was why they were already paying for the coaching, so they could learn. And Carol in return reminded him how often Coach mentioned using professional help. In the end they had found some comfortable middle ground and, as they settled once again in Coach's office, leaving behind the early evening sounds of the city, they were in agreement. They would continue to learn as much as they could but would not risk their enterprise for the sake of a professional fee here or there.

The emotions of the negotiation

"So, you want to buy at a big discount – and you want to buy *fast*, right?"

Coach mischievously opened the session by laying a trap – which, by nodding their agreement, they both fell right into.

"So you apply some gentle pressure on the seller, yes?"

Again they nodded.

"Wrong!" They looked at him in surprise. "Although you'll be looking for people who want to sell fast, hurrying them is the worst thing you can do. In fact, there might even be occasions when you actively discourage them from selling! Surprised by that?"

They nodded silently.

"Thought so. It's all to do with getting a win-win deal, which is what you should always be chasing. You're *not* in the business in order to exploit people. But I will explain and it'll all make perfect sense."

Coach saw that Carol had brought her new ring binder with her. He noticed some more property details and was pleased they were putting in the hours between sessions.

"Now, you should have in your folder the list of Motivated Sellers; can you pull it out? OK. So, these are the people you need to be negotiating with – but how do we find them? Any ideas?"

Carol thought for a moment and then spoke up.

"Well, I guess the estate agent might help?"

"Unlikely!" Steve replied. "They might want a sale, but they won't be so keen on the discount."

"Yes and no," Coach said. "But leave the agents out of it for now. Every time you view a house, you're finding out about the seller. Carol, I see you've got some house details in your file; can you just get one out, it doesn't matter which."

She selected the particulars for a 3-bed semi-detached, 1930's build.

"Good, nice choice. OK, so let's say you've fixed a viewing and the owner's showing you round. You have a fantastic opportunity to ask questions, and as long as you ask the right ones, you'll be able to assess the owner's motivation to sell."

Carol had a question. "But surely, if they're on the ball they might play it cool, especially if they think we're after a big discount. I mean, that's certainly what I would do."

"I don't think Coach means we just go in and say 'you up for a discount for a quick sale mate?'" Steve laughed.

"Actually Steve, that's pretty much what you will say, but as Carol says, not straight away. No, you just get chatting, ask why they're selling, show an interest in their circumstances, be sympathetic. What you *don't* do is go in all hard-nosed and business-like. And the reason for this is absolutely crucial to good negotiating – emotions."

Steve looked down, worried where this might be going.

"Think about it – how many of the reasons on Carol's list of motivated sellers are to do with bad news? These people are going through real emotional experiences, and whatever the reason, their need to sell is closely tied up with it. You might find you're talking to someone who wants to keep it brief and business-like, which is fine and saves a lot of time. But it's more likely the seller has not yet thought about the benefits of selling quickly and without hassle, even if it is at a discount. And if you treat them and their dilemma with respect, they will be far happier dealing with you when they *do* work this out."

Carol spoke up again. "He's right Steve. Remember when you had to sell the old sports car, when our second baby came? Coach, he doted on that car; it was his passion. But we needed a back seat, pure and simple, and money was really tight thanks to new prams and so on. But Steve, you actually turned down two perfectly good offers, do you remember?"

"Yeah, well, they were just after a quick buck; they'd have sold her on like a piece of junk. If I couldn't keep the car any more I was determined to find her a good home."

"Don't tell me – you sold it in the end to some lovely old guy for far less?"

"Well, it was a woman, just divorced, but yes, I just felt I could trust her to look after the old thing."

"There you are then! It's all tied up with emotions! And, it's not actually all that different to any other business. I mean, Steve, when you're deciding where to buy paper and card, I doubt you think of it as an emotional decision?"

Steve almost blushed at the idea.

"But I bet you do factor in loyalty and long-term associations, not just best price? Thought so. It's all to do with integrity, and many owners in a fix will often be much happier dealing with someone they feel they can trust, someone who understands them. And whatever the motivation or need to sell, you can approach the deal with integrity. Whether or not you believe in the saying 'what goes around comes around', it's really important to earn a good reputation in the profession. It always pays off in the end.

"Look at Carol's house again." They looked at the particulars, lying on his desk. "You're viewing it, remember, only now let's say the owner is very tight-lipped, tells you he's just put it on the market to test interest; he says he knows his price and won't take any less. What do you do?"

"Tell him he's wrong? Suggest he's better off selling now at a discount?"

"No. You *understand* where he's at in his own mind. He's not ready to discuss discounts and fast transactions. Or maybe he is, but he's not ready to admit it yet. So you just thank him for his time, log his details and make a note to check up in a couple of months' time. If it's still unsold, he may be open to negotiation and hopefully will have good, positive memories of you from before. This puts you in a much stronger position."

Steve chipped in. "That makes sense, because if he's not going to budge, there'll be no discount, and—"

Carol interrupted; "Without a discount, we've failed at one of the rules and—"

Now Coach leapt in.

"And so you walk away from it. Exactly." He paused, delighted by his protégés.

Carol sucked her pen thoughtfully as she formed a question.

"You said at the start that we might actually *stop* someone from selling? What did you mean?"

"Well, you can't actually stop someone, but I did suggest discouraging them. It's part of the integrity, the win-win goal. You see, as a buyer you're a professional, not a private individual looking for a home. You're also well connected thanks to your expert team – solicitor, mortgage broker and so on. And because you want to sleep easy at night, you're not out to rip anyone off. So, sometimes you might find someone who's scared, getting no sound advice from anyone and is blindly rushing to sell their home when in fact they needn't. There could be other solutions – remortgaging for example – and it may take *you* to help them see this. I'm not suggesting you set yourselves up as Property Angels, saving peoples' homes for them! But as professionals looking for the win-win outcome, sometimes this mean helping them out at no apparent profit to you.

"Let's take a quick break. I want all of this to sink in as it's a big part of the investor's mind-set. It will also help you when you get down to the very final price negotiations. Let's have some coffee!"

Looking for motivated sellers

"OK, so that's how you do it when you've already found a house and are now meeting the owner at the viewing. But it's a bit of a hit-and-miss way to find the motivated seller, so let's do it the other way round; you start off by looking for the *seller* first, and house second. This can save you loads of time and effort."

Steve nodded while Carol wrote notes in her file.

"So – where do you look? Any ideas? No? Well, take a look at this."

Hand-out 3

Finding Motivated sellers	
Other professionals *People you know or deal with on a professional level, and who may hear of keen sellers*	• Letting agents • Financial advisors • Solicitors • Mortgage brokers • Accountants
Advertising *Different methods and different places to advertise*	• Leaflets and cards (house drop, shops etc) • Newspaper advertisements • Billboards • Car boot sales • Car • To Let boards • Text message (to people advertising their house to let) • GP surgery with TV ad screen
Property sourcers *People whose job is to search out properties and sellers*	• Property Sourcing companies

figure 11

Coach handed each of them another list *(figure 11)*, this time giving all kinds of tips for finding motivated sellers.

He carried on talking as they looked through them.

"Some are more obvious than others, and they all require different amounts of input from you. But these are all the techniques that most property companies would use – it's how *we* do it."

He paused, seeing the frowns on both of their faces, and chuckled.

"You both look very worried! You needn't be. No one expects you to do everything on the list. No, you need to find out what works best for the area you're looking in, and what works best for you too. And remember what we learned last session about how to approach the stressed sellers?"

"We talked a lot about that on the way home," Carol explained, "and I think it actually makes the whole idea of approaching people easier – you know, when you understand what they might be going through."

"Good, good," Coach smiled back at her. "Of course, it's a really useful idea to go to some Investor events if you can. You'll meet all kinds of people who, like you, had to start from nowhere and have learned which technique suits them best."

He paused to let them finish reading through the list. Carol spoke up again.

"Looking at some of these, I can't quite see what we actually do."

"OK," Coach replied, "let's take a look – let's start with text messaging. It's very simple. Some people who advertise their house for renting might actually prefer to sell it because of their circumstances. So all you do is send a text message saying 'we will buy your house and give you 70% of its value. We are serious buyers and can complete within 3 weeks.'"

Steve sniggered. "I'd tell someone to take a running jump if I got a text like that!"

"Well, most people do assuming they bother to respond, but one or two will be interested. It only costs about £3 a week to send the texts, and even if it only turns up one sale every three months, it's worth it!"

"OK, so what about To Let boards?" Steve asked.

"Ah," Coach smiled, "this is really clever. At my company we have our own To Let boards and once a property is let, the council allows you to keep the board up for another month. Now, most agents simply replace the To Let board with one that says 'property now let' and gives their phone number. We put up a board that says 'We will buy your house for cash guaranteed – call this number'."

"Oh I see, so really it's grabbing an opportunity to put up an advertisement?"

"Exactly. And talking of advertisements, you can always put these in the local paper; you'll see property companies doing this and it can work very well."

"OK," Steve replied, "I get it now; all of these are just ways of letting potential sellers know we're there—"

"And that you're a serious buyer ready to complete in record time!" Coach added.

"Yes of course. I was just thinking, as we run a printing firm, we could print our own cards and leaflets."

"Quite," Coach agreed, "but remember, successful advertising is a skill; there's a lot to learn and it might be a good idea for you both to go on a course? We run them if you're interested; just go to our website www.propertyinsight.

co.uk and look up courses. In fact," he looked over his glasses, "I suggest you make this your principal homework for this session; that, and looking up some Investor Clubs and events. I'm really keen to get you out there meeting and networking as soon as possible."

They looked a little happier, reassured by the idea of friendly support.

"Good. Now, there's one technique you might like to think about and it relates to the very first guy on the list, the estate agent. Instead of hand-picking individual properties and arranging to view, you make an offer on, let's say, 25 properties, and all at 30% below the asking price. You won't even have seen the properties but, you see, the agent is legally obliged to put your offers forward to the sellers. Most sellers will come back with a firm 'no' but you could well get one or two showing interest. It feels a bit like a bull in a china shop, but it saves a heck of a lot of time!"

Coach closed his file causing Carol to look at her watch.

"No, we haven't quite finished; I want to end today with a little role play." He smiled at Steve's look of alarm.

Closing the deal

Carol was intrigued. She was generally up for most things, but she was a bit worried for Steve, knowing how much he hated this kind of thing. As it turned out, she needn't have worried.

"Right, I'm going to try to buy the same house from each of you in turn, OK? And one of you will sell but the other won't. Don't worry – the sale that doesn't work will be my fault. I'll being showing you a couple of different ways to negotiate a deal. So, who'd like to go first?"

There was no question of Steve volunteering so Carol put herself forward.

"Now, your house is on the market for £100,000, OK? Here we go – are you ready?"

She nodded.

"*So, we've been chatting for a few minutes, and then I make my offer* – Given the state of the market, you really should try to sell fast, so tell you what, I'll offer you £70,000; it's a fair price and—"

"Sorry, no way. I might be able to go down a bit, but certainly not 30%!"

"OK – can't blame a man for trying; how about £80,000, my last offer?"

He put his hand up to stop Carol from replying.

"Let's just pause – now, what have I just done?"

Steve looked confused.

"Well, I came in at £70,000, bit cheeky but always worth a go. Then immediately I leapt up ten grand, 10%. What message does that give to Carol?"

"Er – that if she holds firm you'll go up another ten?"

"Exactly. And if I do, bang goes my minimum 15% discount! So what should I have done?"

Carol spoke up this time.

"Stuck firm at £70,000. I was bound to say no to begin with and might have come round—"

"Interesting – and actually, there's a lot of sense in offering one figure and leaving it there, particularly if you are offering on multiple similar properties. One of them might bite, which then saves you the hassle of viewing and negotiating with the others. But what if you didn't want to leave it there, what if you really wanted to try for *this* house? Let's try again, but why not swop? Steve, it's now you selling the house. Here we go."

Steve shuffled in his chair, nervous but keen to see how this panned out.

"Right – nice house blah blah – my offer on the table is £70,000. What do you say?"

"Well, I agree with Carol – I'm not interested."

"OK – let me think – what about £72,000? I really can't go much further …"

"Well, sorry, but I simply can't drop the price that much."

" (Assume that we now have a discussion about the market going quiet, me being a serious buyer, able to complete in four weeks, blah blah blah   in other words, I've engaged you in conversation and you're listening. This means I have a chance – you haven't just shown me the door – OK back into role) – Well, I realise you were hoping for more but I'm serious – tell you what, the most I can push it to would be £72,250."

Up went Coach's hand once more to pause the dialogue.

"Carol – what do you think Steve's thinking now?"

She looked at her husband and could see in his eyes that he was doing sums in his mind.

"He's thinking figures – I don't know – probably working out if it's enough to clear what he owes?"

"Steve?"

Steve grinned and nodded.

"Thought so – you see, by engaging you and *then* throwing in a silly number, not leaping up in tens of thousands, I've helped you forget the £100,000 and instead you're trying to evaluate my latest offer in relation to your situation. And your come-back might be …?"

"£80,000 – my bottom line."

"It's a deal!" Coach laughed. "And it was *you*, the seller, who came up with the final figure so you felt you were in control of the negotiation. And I get my 20% discount which makes me very happy."

Steve looked as though he'd fallen into a trap, so Coach explained.

"Remember, the seller will have the next four weeks to reconsider, to wonder if he's made a mistake and possibly to pull out – which is the last thing you want. That's why it's so important that the seller feels he controlled the negotiation and picked the final price. We'll come back to this next time when we talk about looking after the seller through the final steps. But does that make sense now?"

Steve nodded. Coach stood up, looking at the clock.

"My, we've overrun, I'm sorry. For homework I want you to do just one thing; find some time together and talk your way through the list I gave you about finding motivated sellers. You need to agree which methods you feel most confident using as new buyers. And you mustn't fall into the trap of feeling sorry for the seller. You can help by buying their house but *only* if the price is right, and that means at least 15% off the true market value, remember!"

They both sat quietly, looking very serious. Coach laughed.

"Don't worry! It's just business, OK? And I'll be giving you a list of useful books which teach all kinds of negotiating techniques. For now I just want you to get into the right mind-set."

Coach closed the folder on his desk.

"Now, I have an Investor's Club meeting to address, and I'm late. 'Til next time."

8. Purchasing: your Power Team

- **The right team**
- **Ready to act**
- **Don't forget the vendor!**

"Oh Steve, for goodness sake – park anywhere!" Carol was impatient to see Coach. Following his advice last time they had set aside an entire evening to talk through the list of motivated sellers. It had been a revelation, both in what now seemed so obvious, the range of circumstances sellers find themselves in, and in the focus it gave to their own motivation as investors.

"Look, if we come out later and find we've got a ticket, you're paying, OK?" Steve's day had been fraught with supplier problems and Carol, busy preparing for a VAT inspection, hadn't been much help. To cap it all he was missing the snooker on TV. Maybe his motivation *was* sagging after all, but Carol knew he'd pick up once the session started. Although she hadn't said anything, secretly she was amazed by his enthusiasm and particularly his grasp of the investor mind-set – she even wondered if this revealed an alter ego, hidden until now.

"Sure," she agreed, "just as long as we're not late. We've got so much to tell Coach tonight – I just can't wait to see his face."

The right team

Coach had only just arrived when Carol and Steve knocked on the door.

"Come in, come in!" he called out cheerfully. After his own long day overseeing four property refurbishments, he was looking forward to an hour or so in the company of his keen tutees.

"So, been practising your negotiation skills, Steve? Have you managed to slash paper and card costs?"

"Don't mention supplies!" Carol begged. "He's had a terrible day."

"Oh, I'm sorry to hear that. You'll find it much easier negotiating over property you know, if you stick to the rules. Now, today—"

"Actually," Carol interrupted, "we've done something since we last saw you." She was almost fizzing with excitement now that she could at last tell him. "We went to our first networking event. I know maybe we jumped the gun but—"

"Nonsense! For a moment I thought you were going to say you'd bought a house, but no, I'm absolutely delighted to hear it. I think all the investment networking groups are good. I know that PIN[8] operates in many towns across the country – and their education is spot on. The important thing is that you can learn so much from other investors, so the sooner you join a group the better. Some of my students feel they can't even go for a taster visit until they've 'finished the course' – I tell them this isn't a 'course', just a pointer to what they still need to learn, but they don't understand. So, you went; good for you – tell me more … "

"It was Steve's idea really, a client he spoke to – well, you tell him Steve."

....

8 Property Investor's Networking – one of the networking groups you can join

"Yes," Steve picked up the story, "it was a coincidence really." And he went on to describe the conversation that began with promotional gift pens and ended up with overseas holiday investment apartments. The client had joined a club that specialised in new-build holiday lets, and although Carol put her foot down the moment Steve relayed this to her, it had given him the idea to find a local network group.

"Well, once again, I'm impressed and pleased for you both. It really is one of the best ways to learn, and to find help if things go wrong too. Now then, unless you're now so well-connected you've decided to give me the boot," he chuckled, "we need to push on." They got themselves ready, Carol with notepad and Steve with calculator.

"I don't think you'll need that today Steve – we're going to look at the process of actually purchasing the property; but remember, we've done the negotiating, so the price is more or less worked out. *Purchasing*," he emphasised, "is all about good project management – and most of all about people."

"Now, wouldn't it be great if buying a property was no harder than – say – buying a car? And certainly," Coach smiled at Steve, "easier than *selling* one!" Steve grinned.

"Well, it can be, providing you have everything – and everyone – in place. You need what I call your 'Power Team', primed and ready to leap into action. So, tell me – who do you think should be in this team?"

It wasn't a hard question and they both fired their answers together.

"Mortgage broker"… "Surveyor"… "Accountant"… "Solicitor"…

"Good, that's actually only about a third of them, but it'll do for now. Of course, as people already running a business, you've probably got at least two of these in place, yes?"

"Sure – we've got an accountant and our solicitor, both great guys—"

"Don't forget the mortgage broker, Steve. We changed our mortgage a couple of years ago," Carol explained to Coach, "and I'm sure she's still working in the same branch."

Coach sat silent for a few seconds looking at them, and then removed his glasses.

"Interesting, but I wonder ... this sports car, Steve, it sounds as though you treasured it, yes? So tell me, for servicing and repairs, where did you take it? The same place that did your vans?"

"No way!" Steve protested. "I found this amazing mechanic who got to know every inch of her, could tell what was wrong just by listening to the engine. Do you know, he—"

Carol dug him in the ribs, knowing he'd talk for hours about the old car given a chance. Coach tried not to smile.

"Well, that's exactly what you do as an investor. I'm sure you have excellent professionals in place for buying your own home, but that's not what you're doing here is it? It's all part of the right mind-set – and being ready to work with the experts."

Nodding, Steve turned to Carol. "He's right. Think about Debbie – isn't that her name? She was recommended to us as a whizz kid with domestic mortgages. What *you* are saying, Coach, is that we now need someone who specialises in buy to let mortgages?"

"Exactly. Same goes for your accountant and your solicitor. Financially it's a completely different landscape, with different products to choose from, and legally you need someone in place who knows all the pitfalls. But how are you going to find and recruit these experts? Carol?"

Carol thought for a moment, then beamed as she made a connection. "At networking events!"

"Yes – that's one way; the other is simply to ask about their own property portfolios. If they don't have one, they're almost definitely not the right experts for you."

"But, what if they won't tell us? I mean, it's personal information, and I remember one of the IFAs we saw, he refused to tell us what *he* was investing in even though I thought it was such an obvious question to ask."

"Well, if they won't talk about it, they're not the right people are they? You'll find that most successful investors are perfectly happy to discuss their portfolios and experience. You should be able to see their accounts or bank statements showing their rent rolls. And they'll understand why you're asking. If they don't, they're probably not the right people to be dealing with."

Coach noticed that Steve was looking into the distance, thinking. "Steve, what's on your mind?"

"Oh – sorry, I was just thinking about whether our solicitor would feel snubbed if we used a different one for the portfolio purchases. But of course it's a really useful way to keep personal and business matters separate, which you keep advising us to do. No, I've no problem finding the right people – God knows, we'll be paying them enough!"

"That's the right attitude!" Coach laughed.

"Now, before we tackle the next critical aspect of purchasing, I just want you to think about *one* member of your power team, the surveyor or valuer."

"I've never quite known what the difference is between them," Steve commented. Coach laughed.

"That's easy – there isn't one, not really. They both do the same thing – put a value on the property *and* tell you if it's about to fall down!"

"But don't they act on the bank's behalf? How can they be on our side, in our team?" Carol asked.

"True," Coach replied, "the bank's surveyor is there to compare the buying price with their own valuation to make sure the bank doesn't lend too much. So if they know what you're paying, they tend to value it for the same figure, ignoring the fact that you got it at a discount. What *you* need is a survey that confirms you're paying the right price – the investor's price."

"So how do we get that?" Steve asked. "We can't start bribing surveyors!"

Coach laughed. "No, and why would you? You're after the true figure, not one that happens to suit you. No, you pay for an additional but independent survey. Say there's a property on at £100,000, and you negotiate a discounted price of £80k. The bank's surveyor, knowing this, will almost always value it at £80,000. So based on that alone, you don't know for sure if you're paying a good price or not. Now, you send in your own surveyor, with a blank sheet of paper if you like, and the outcome is a true valuation of £95,000. 15% off that is—"

"Exactly," Steve interrupted, punching the '=' button on his calculator, "£80,750."

"So, your offer of £80,000 is spot on for the 15% discount off true value. Had it shown that you were only getting, say, 10% discount, you would then have pulled out of the deal. And all you'd lose is the small £150 fee for the independent survey."

"So what you're saying is that while a solicitor will fight our corner even if we're pushing for a daft price, our surveyor is there to give us an accurate picture, plain and simple?" Carol asked, scribbling notes as she spoke.

"That's right. And for peace of mind, two tips: firstly, you *can* get what's called a desktop valuation for as little as £15 – Hometrack is one of the companies that do this for you – but as you can now see, £150 buys you a hell of a lot more peace of mind." He paused to let Carol catch up before continuing. "Secondly, it's good practice to use the same surveyors that buy to let mortgage companies use – then they talk the same language and it avoids complications."

Ready to act

Coach paused to let all this sink in before continuing.

"OK – any questions about the power team?"

"Yes – you said there were others, that this was only a third of the team," Steve stated.

"You're correct but I'll come to the remainder another day when we discuss refurbishing. You see, the others are all builders and tradespeople; you often won't need them until you have ownership of the property."

Steve understood.

"But the next vital lesson, now you have your purchasing team in place, is to make sure they are all ready to leap into action. Remember when we talked about negotiation – I said you must never rush the seller, yes? But I also mentioned that promising a quick completion can be a deal-maker? Well, in that scenario you should aim to complete the entire purchase in only four weeks from your offer being accepted."

Carol's eyebrows went up. "Four weeks? It took longer than that just to sort out the new mortgage!"

"Actually, four weeks is a maximum. You should aim to do it in less, and with investment property it's perfectly possible. Which is exactly why you need a specialist broker, you see," Coach reiterated. "But not just any specialist; you need one who can act as soon as you press 'go'. It's no good having someone in mind, getting your offer accepted and then finding they're fully booked or on holiday – you could lose two weeks just finding a replacement."

"But even if we have one, and we tell them we're putting in an offer, we can't know for sure when the offer will be accepted?" Carol was sceptical that anything could work quite so smoothly.

"No, you can't, so you just have to be as organised as possible. Remember, good professionals don't actually like letting clients down. But once everything does kick off, you must keep in regular contact with each member of your team. You need to be the first to be told if *anything* crops up and threatens a delay."

"Which, let's face it, is what happens in the real world." Steve shared his wife's doubts.

"No, you need to be really clear on this; with the right people, the right team, you *can* complete everything on time. The only reason private houses take so long is because people tend to haggle or delay over prices, and they're dealing with chains that break and so on. And of course," he smiled at them, "solicitors, agents – in fact any of them – they're not usually known for their speed! So if you're at all worried I would advise once again that you ask a property company, or why not chat to some serious investors at the next group meeting? They should each have a list of tried and tested people they can recommend."

Don't forget the vendor!

"Right," Coach looked at a hand-written list on his desk, "I must say, we're getting through today's agenda very smoothly. You should find that each new topic now gets easier to grasp – particularly as you are both thinking with the mind-set of investors."

They both nodded agreement.

"OK, the last lesson in purchasing involves the other crucial person – the seller. What do think is happening in their world while you chase up your power team? What's going through their mind – any ideas?"

"Relief I should think!" Steve suggested. Coach smiled.

"You'd think so wouldn't you? But that's not always the case, especially if you achieved a substantial discount (which of course you should, otherwise why are you buying the property?). Four weeks – that's twenty-eight long days; more than enough time to have second thoughts, to be down the pub having your ear bent about the stupid price you agreed, to be told off for not hanging on for another buyer. Or – there could be other offers; you might suddenly find you're out of the picture."

"But surely they agreed to sell precisely because they trust us and know we'll not mess them around?"

"Oh yes – and the offer that gazumps yours may well fall through in the end, but an already stressed seller, now with a full four weeks to reflect, is under a lot of pressure. So, what do you do to prevent any of this happening? Carol?"

"Erm – you could get your solicitor to write something reassuring I suppose, to show you are serious?"

"Not necessary," Coach replied bluntly. "Why pay your solicitor when you can do the same thing yourself? No, *you* keep in touch with the seller; make contact every three days, keep them up to speed with how things are going. That's rule number one. The other rule is to offer help. It's very likely that they are not nearly as well prepared as you are. For example, you can't both use the same solicitor but you can still recommend one that you trust to do the work punctually and to maintain excellent communication should anything go wrong."

"I see, and this won't seem like us interfering then?" Steve asked.

"Well, you're only offering aren't you? They don't have to accept your help; but if it's in their own interests to complete fast, they will probably be grateful for any assistance they can get."

"And I suppose," Carol jumped in, "it's all part of staying in touch as well. It shows we are all after the same thing, a pain-free and swift completion."

"Exactly. You're almost like business partners in the transaction. Speaking of which – I need *your* agreement on something."

They both looked up expectantly.

"Do you agree – we should break for coffee?" He grinned at them both.

"Sure – I could do with a breather," Steve said enthusiastically before adding, "But is that everything then for Purchasing? No hand-outs?"

Coach laughed. "No hand-outs, and yes, that covers the basics. What we have to look at next is far more complicated – financing your purchase – but first I need to recharge the old brain with some caffeine; and Steve, we'll be doing some serious number crunching so I hope your batteries are fully charged too!"

9. Financing your property purchases

- **Leverage**
- **Buy to let mortgages**
- **Raising the deposit**
- **Refinancing and growing your portfolio**

Their coffee break was longer than usual thanks to an urgent message on Carol's phone from the babysitter. It turned out to be a false alarm – Peter definitely did *not* have a nut allergy; having inherited his father's mischievousness, he'd simply been trying it on.

"I'm so sorry," said Carol, "his best friend at school has just been diagnosed with an allergy and now it's become the latest excuse for getting out of anything and everything."

"No worries," Coach smiled, "it shows a certain resourcefulness – and if that's a family trait I'm pleased because it's exactly what you're going to need for the last topic tonight – finance."

Steve gave that look again, the one he used whenever money and accounts were mentioned.

"Don't worry Steve – this isn't going to be all about figures and percentages – well it is, but it's more about being *creative,* being *innovative* … right up your street!"

"Right, you remember early on we talked about leverage, yes? Well, I just want to bring it up again as it's the most important financial aspect of good investing – using someone else's money to make your own work harder."

"I love it when you say that; it's the first time I've ever thought of borrowing money as something to celebrate!" Steve joked.

"Well it's true, and it's very simple to demonstrate."

Coach paused, opened one of his desk drawers and pulled out a stapler, a hole punch, a box of rubber bands and a handful of paperclips. He carefully counted out eight of the paperclips and pushed them across towards Carol and Steve.

"Now, that's your money OK? All you've got are eight, and your plan is to build a portfolio of three properties. And I just happen to have three very desirable properties," he gestured grandly at the assorted pieces of equipment on the desk, "but there's one problem – each one costs eight paperclips. So what do you do?"

"That's easy – we put down what we've got and borrow the rest. If the total cost is twenty-four paperclips and we've got eight, then we borrow the other sixteen from the bank."

"You can – but that means you're putting down a 33% deposit – and the bank's happy with only 25%, so why put in more than you have to?"

"But then we have some left over," Carol said, spotting a flaw in Coach's argument, "and you've been telling us we should make our money work – surely leaving it lying around isn't doing that?"

"Who said anything about it lying around?" Coach replied. "Pay your 25% – which is two paperclips per property —" he paused, remembering the last time he'd played this game; he'd given out only six paperclips and they'd argued about whether you could split a paperclip in half. Pleased he hadn't made the same mistake again he carried on.

" — so with your two paperclips left over, you have enough for a deposit on a *fourth* property. And," he opened his draw again and, pulling out a phone charger, he placed it in front of them, "I have just the property you're looking for." He beamed, seeing them smiling at his little game.

"The point is, a professional property investor will keep as little personal money in the portfolio as possible but make it work hard. Your equity will grow and this is useful if you are still expanding your portfolio, and we'll look at that shortly. But the basic principle is to control as valuable an asset as you can with as little of your own money in it as possible."

"So are you saying we never pay off these mortgages then?" Steve was confused.

"For as long as we're talking about you *controlling* an asset, not *owning* it, then yes. If you pay it off, then you own the property but this actually means you have loads of capital sitting in the form of bricks and mortar, money that could instead be financing several additional houses—"

"—as a 25% deposit in each! I've got it." Steve looked pleased.

Coach was relieved. "Don't worry, it's just that old home-owner mind-set creeping back in – the instinct to pay off your debts. Remember, the investment mortgage is a good debt, not something to fear or do battle with."

Steve grinned, imagining knights in armour riding into the building society office.

"In fact," Coach peered into his folder, "I have a really good diagram to explain this, but I'll give it out at the end of the session when we look more closely at refinancing. For now, it's a good moment to clarify the relationship between mortgage payments and rental income. It's something many new investors worry about."

Carol looked back through her notes, locating her section on 'rent'. She looked up to show she was ready.

"The rent you charge and the size of your mortgage are linked – and it's all worked out for you as the lender will only lend according to one simple calculation. You must be able to charge rent of at least 125% of your mortgage repayment; so if you repay £400 a month, you must be able to charge at least £500 a month in rent."

Carol looked up, smiling. "Ah – that explains something that was bugging me. We've talked about increasing the mortgage to draw off some income, but I had wondered how we'd meet the higher repayments. I'd guessed we could put up the rents to cover the increase – now I see in fact we have to, in order to comply with the lender's rules?"

"That's pretty much it," Coach replied, "and be warned; there are just two main rules for buy to let mortgages – this 125% rent to mortgage one, and the minimum 25% deposit one. Bear in mind though," Coach gave them one of his serious looks over the spectacles, "the lender will base their calculations on their own valuer's valuation or on what you are paying, whichever is the *lower* figure. You can't just bung in whatever figure suits your sums! Also, the more equity you have, the greater the choice of mortgages."

Buy to let mortgages

"Now, before I show you this, a word of warning," Coach announced solemnly. "I keep talking about 75% mortgages – but as the financial world gets stronger once again, lenders will start to offer 85% mortgages. However, don't be tempted! Stick to 75% and then, should things get tough again, you have what I call an Equity Buffer to protect you if the property value dips for a while."

Coach then gave them both a handout *(figure 12)*. On it were definitions and details of the different types of buy to let mortgage.

Hand-out 4

Buy to Let Mortgages

LTV – Loan to Value	LTV = % of the property's value that the lender will lend to you.
	Currently most mortgages are offered at 75% LTV (e.g. £60k on a property valued at £80k).
	Some lenders might offer lower LTV (eg 60%); these can charge lower interest rates BUT you have to put more of your own money into the property. You need this money to go towards the next property, so 75%LTV is advised.
Fixed vs Tracker mortgages	Fixed: the interest rate is fixed for a specified period (e.g. 2 years).
	Tracker: the rate goes up or down whenever the Bank of England base rate changes – it tracks the base rate.
Interest-only vs Repayment	Interest-only mortgage: your monthly repayments only cover the interest on the loan. At the end of the mortgage term (e.g. 25 years) you still owe the original capital sum borrowed (e.g. £75k against a house valued at £100k).
	Repayment mortgage: each month you repay part of the interest and part of the capital. At the end of the mortgage term the entire loan is paid off.
	For Buy to Let, interest-only mortgages are strongly recommended for greater tax-efficiency.

You should always consult a mortgage broker when making decision about loans. Your networking group may include a broker experienced in Buy to Let purchases. And if not, someone in the group will probably be able to recommend brokers to you.

figure 12

Raising the deposit

- **Savings**
- **Loans**
- **Equity**
- **Joint venturing**

"Now" Coach said with a glimmer in his eye, "time to get creative!" and, pushing aside the clutter on his desk, he replaced it with a single, clean piece of paper.

Steve shuffled uncomfortably. He'd survived the role-play the other day but was not sure what would be expected now.

Savings

"Where can you find that magical 25% deposit that makes the property yours? Any ideas?"

Carol spoke first. "Savings? Or perhaps an inheritance?"

Coach scribbled these both down on the paper. "Both good. Saving of course takes a long time, but if you start early on it's surprising how quickly it accumulates. And an inheritance? Well imagine you inherited £25,000. It's a strange amount – not enough to pay off your own mortgage perhaps, and too much to blow on a holiday – but just enough to kick-start your portfolio!"

"What do you think, Carol? Who have we got in the family who might leave us £25,000?" Steve joked.

"Of course there are other ways that family members can help though," Coach continued, "by lending you the money or joining you in a joint venture. Let's just think about loans first."

Loans

Carol and Steve glanced at each other, thinking of some of the notoriously mean distant members of both their families. Coach added 'loans' to his list.

"The one thing I always stress to anyone thinking of borrowing from family – or from friends for that matter – is to become an expert *first*. You must know what you're doing, and how the maths works. If you're on top of it all, you will know exactly what your lender can expect to get in return. And if you have a solid agreement in place covering who makes decisions and who gets what, you should be OK. Without these, you'll be heading for one almighty bust-up."

"It's not the people who are the problem for us, it's that no one has very much money as far as we know," Steve explained.

"Sometimes that's the main reason why you *should* think about family. If you can get 30% return on the investment, wouldn't it be nice to share that around? If enough of you pool together, you can all enjoy proportional shares of the profit. But of course that raises questions of who actually owns the portfolio. Much simpler would be to borrow the money for a short term, just until you're in a position to refinance. Say you borrow the deposit, £25,000, and buy at the right discount; and over a six month period your property value goes up enough for you to refinance and release the £27,500 back in cash. You then pay this back to the family lender giving them a 10% return within less than a year – not bad at all! And it's meant you've got into property investing without having to put down your own deposit. It's win-win, and all thanks to the power of making profits through leverage!"

"OK," Carol responded, "it makes sense, but what if we don't want to involve the family at all, and we don't want to use up all our savings; do we borrow the deposit as a personal loan?"

Steve shot a sharp glance towards her. He wasn't great at saving money in an organised way but was dead against taking out any more bank loans than they had to.

"Well," began Coach, "it's an option, and some people do use personal loans or even their credit cards. The danger, obviously, is that you end up unable to afford the repayments. But I suppose if, say, you're someone with a £10,000 credit card facility, repayable at 0% over 18 months, and your strategy means you are confident of clearing the debt, you could make it work."

"Or perhaps," Carol had another idea, "we could have some kind of business loan so that repayments came from the business – I mean, we're doing well enough aren't we Steve?"

"No way," Steve insisted. "We're not doing anything if it puts the business at risk."

Carol shrugged, knowing that deep down she agreed with Steve.

"Just remember it's a personal choice," Coach concluded.

Equity

"Of course," Coach added another item to his list, "you will probably have some useful equity in your own house – with that you can take out a mortgage and use it as the deposit. Many people do."

Carol drew a sharp breath, not keen on mixing private and portfolio finances. Coach laughed.

"I know, you don't like the sound of that. But it's fine, just as long as—"

"—we do the maths? Yes I know ..." Carol laughed.

"It's *also* one way that some people arrange to pay off their own mortgage early. I can show you this with a simple illustration – based on very conservative figures because I know you prefer to see the glass as half empty rather than half full." He glanced at Steve who pulled a miserable face in return.

"Let's say your own house is worth £300,000, with a £100,000 mortgage on it. You want to buy a portfolio worth £400,000, so you need a 25% deposit of £100,000. You raise this by increasing your own mortgage by £100,000 and use that money as the deposit. You now have a £200,000 mortgage on your own home, and you control four investment properties worth £400,000 in all, £300,000 of which is covered by your buy to let mortgages."

Steve, at last able to punch some figures into his calculator, looked up waiting for the next ones.

"OK," Coach continued, "now being conservative, let's say that over the next ten years, the value doesn't double but goes up by only 50%. Where does that leave us?

"Our own house is now worth £450,000," Steve replied, "and the portfolio has gone up to £600,000."

"That's right. Now, let's suppose that the mortgages are all interest-only, as I always recommend. You now decide to sell the portfolio for £600,000, pay off the £300,000 mortgage and the £100,000 mortgage extension on your own home, and – "

"We have £200,000 profit!" Steve announced.

"Or," Carol interrupted, "we then repay our original £100,000 mortgage – and we're debt free and still have £100,000 in the bank!"

"Exactly," Coach said. "But – I don't want to encourage you just to do that; you're here to become professional property investors for the long term. This just shows you how you can use leverage to grow amazing profits in ten lean years. Imagine what you can do if you allow your portfolio to keep growing, and we hit financially better times again!"

Joint venturing

"Now, you've already been to a networking group haven't you?" They nodded. "I wonder – did anyone announce they were looking for joint venture partners?"

Steve grinned. "Yes, I thought they were looking for someone to finance a new holiday block in Bulgaria or somewhere!"

Coach laughed. "They might well have been. More likely though that they're doing exactly what you're planning, building up a portfolio more locally! You see, two things to remember – one, we're approaching your investment as a business, and two, there are an awful lot of people with *some* money to spare who have the same goals as yourselves. So for anyone struggling to find enough deposit money, pooling your resources makes a lot of sense – and that's joint venturing. And you can divide up the responsibilities too – one side puts in more money but does less of the work, that kind of thing."

"Hmm," Steve said, "sounds to me as risky as getting family members involved. People are bound to fall out, and then what happens to it all?"

"That's why you have a well worked out agreement covering everything, including what happens if someone needs to pull out. It's something your specialist property lawyer can help you with, or you can get advice from other investors."

Carol spoke up. "But how do you know if you can trust someone? I mean we're now talking about complete strangers. In fact, why should anyone trust *us?*"

"Good question," Coach replied. "And my answer is the same as for dealing with family – *you* need to know what you're talking about. And you two already know a lot more than many at this early stage. Just think how much we've covered so far!"

Steve looked reassured by this. "I guess so," he said, "and now we're going to networking events as well – so yes, I see what you mean. I bet there are people out there who just leap in with no idea. People who," and he leaned away from Carol as he said this, "would go out and buy the first four houses they liked, for all the wrong reasons." Carol just glowered at him.

"Of course, without wanting to dent your confidence, there's a lot more still to learn!" Coach warned them. "And if you wanted to look for venture partners, you would certainly need to do some extra study – there's a great book by Simon Zutshi[9] which talks about venturing partnerships, and any good property company can give you a lot of help too. In fact, there are also excellent books by Rob Moore and Mark Homer – all well worth reading. The thing is, just remember that joint venturing can be a good option if you're struggling to find sufficient deposit money."

"Do you know, Steve, I'm quite interested in the idea of a joint venture," Carol mused. "Of course, we'd have to choose a partner very carefully."

"Yes – I'm not so sure," Steve replied, "I can see all of these ideas are good. But I think we're lucky because we can use the equity in our own house. We could save the other options for some time in the future if we needed some cash injection."

Coach nodded approvingly at their ideas.

....
9 See chapter 20: Useful resources.

Refinancing and growing your portfolio

It was that moment in the session when concentration began to wane. Coach had cunningly accounted for this.

"Now for the best bit," he announced, "playing Monopoly."

They were too tired to do anything other than smile weakly at this.

"Of course I'm joking; saying the word 'monopoly' at an investor's club is like using the 'Macbeth' word inside a theatre – you don't! But you *do* need to know how to grow your portfolio, adding more properties. You came here because you have an eye to the future, more time, less work, good income. So we're looking at investment plans that take time to reach maturity, to grow to their full size. And the secret is to be aggressive when you remortgage and release equity gains, using these as deposits for the next purchases."

"Aggressive finance – sounds a bit dodgy to me," Steve said

"Nonsense, if you don't like the word 'aggressive', think of 'strategic' instead. Now, where's that hand-out I mentioned?" He leafed through his folder and then drew out two copies of a table full of figures *(figure 13)*. Handing a copy to each of them, he explained.

"This is a comprehensive investment model, showing exactly how the refinancing works."

They were both frowning at their sheets, trying to work out what it all meant, so Coach helped them out.

"It's much simpler than it looks," he explained. "Start at the top of each column and work downwards. The columns are the key years in your portfolio's growth when you refinance the property you already own to release cash as the deposit for new properties. And here," he pointed to the far left column, "it

Hand-out 5	Year 1	Year 4
Market value per individual property	100,000	120,000
Action	Buy house value 100,000 for discount at 85,000	Portfolio value up to 120,000 remortgage for 90,000 (75%
Release cash as deposit for new properties (new mortgage total less old mortgage total)		26,000
Buy new property		1 house value 120,000, disc price 102,000 mortgage (75 76,500; depc 25,500
Surplus cash		500
Total mortgages	64,000	166,500
Total personal money invested	21,000	21,000
Number of properties	1	2
Value of portfolio	**100,000**	**240,000**
OR stop growing the portfolio and refinance for an annual income of 3.75% of total asset value	3,750 (refinancing 1 property)	9,000 (refinancing 2 properties)

figure 13

	Year 6	Year 8	Year 12	Year 16
	,000	145,000	176,000	214,000
	folio value o 264,000; ortgage for ,000	Portfolio value up to 435,000; remortgage for 326,000	Portfolio value up to 704,000; remortgage for 528,000	Portfolio value up to 1,498,000; remortgage for 1,123,500
	500	44,000	110,000	285,500
	use value ,000, ount ,000; itional gage 000; deposit 000	1 house value 145,000, discount 123,000; additional mortgage 92,000; deposit 31,000	3 houses, total value 528,000, discount 450,000; additional mortgage 337,500; deposit 112,500	5 houses, total value 1,070,000, discount 909,500; additional mortgage 682,000; deposit 207,500
	0	13,000	10,500	61,500
	,000	418,000	865,000	1,805,000
	000	21,00	21,000	21,000
		4	7	12
	000	**580,000**	**1,232,000**	**2,568,000**
	50 ancing 3 erties)	21,750 (refinancing 4 properties)	46,200 (refinancing 7 properties)	96,300 (refinancing 12 properties)

explains each action that takes place and the impact on your asset growth."

"Wow," Steve was very impressed, "suddenly it all makes sense, everything you've said about leverage, not having to use your own money – and it's really exciting to see the critical moments when you can almost double your portfolio just by refinancing!"

Coach smiled, glad to see the table was revitalising their energy, just as he'd predicted.

"One last thing to point out is the very bottom row; this shows the income you can draw down if you decide to stop adding new properties and just stick with what you've got."

Carol ran her finger along the bottom of her sheet. "I see, so we could decide, for example, to stop in year twelve when we've built it up to seven properties. And the cash we could draw down each year through refinancing those seven is …"

"£46,200!" Steve finished off her sentence. "We could almost retire on that!"

Glancing at his watch, Coach realised they had overrun and he had one last small point to cover.

"Now, before you go home and celebrate the wisdom of your decision in coming to see me," he grinned at his own cheek, "there's one thing you must be aware of, and it's this. Since 2009, there has been a rule stating that when you buy a house, regardless of whether it's a cash purchase or on a mortgage, you *cannot refinance it for the first six months.*"

"That's a bit unfair isn't it?" Carol asked.

"It depends whose side you're on! You see, before this rule was introduced you could buy a £100,000 house at discount for £70,000 cash one day and then take out a mortgage on it the very next day for £75,000, the 75% LTV. And of course that meant the investor had got £25,000 of equity in the property itself *and* £5,000 cash in the bank. The lender meanwhile gained little and hoped that the valuation was correct! So, that's why the rule was introduced, and with the six month delay on refinancing, it's more important than ever that you buy for the right discount."

Carol looked up thoughtfully. "And I suppose that's why the valuation is so critical? Both parties – investor and lender – need to be confident in the property's real value, regardless of the discount we get."

"Exactly," Coach agreed, "and not just confident, but in *agreement* when you go back to remortgage in six months' time. You see, let's say you buy at 30% discount for £70,000 with a mortgage; that means your deposit is £17,500 with the mortgage covering the other £52,500. After six months you need to able to refinance at full value, £100,000, getting a revised mortgage of £75,000. Deduct the original mortgage of £52,500 and the difference more than covers your original deposit. And this is how you can then walk away without leaving any of your own money in property number one and with a deposit ready to use for property number two. This is what it's all about but obviously it relies on the lender agreeing about the value, so you need to be able to back up your figure. That's why it's so important to get an independent valuation when you buy – a record of its value from the start – and also keep receipts of any work you've done to improve the property."

"And if they won't agree?" Steve asked anxiously.

"If you have the records I've just mentioned, that shouldn't happen. It's something you have to learn to do because you need to be releasing and recycling that initial deposit to buy another property every six months or so."

He paused to let Carol scribble some notes.

"So," Coach concluded, "a very full session, lots to take in. I suggest you go through it all carefully and bring any questions to me next time. Not too many though, as we're going to be discussing refurbishment – more creativity!" He chuckled and stood, gesturing them kindly to the door.

10. Coffee break

OK, we're half-way through the book – a good moment to leave Coach and his students while we recap on what we've learned so far.

The hardest task Coach had was at the start. Unless Steve and Carol could adjust their attitudes and preconceptions, he wasn't going to achieve very much; but they *did* change. At the beginning, all they really knew was what Phil had said and what they'd seen on TV programmes like Property Ladder. With Coach's help, they soon began to see a well-managed property portfolio in terms of a *long-term, high yield investment.* Crucially, they grasped important concepts like 'good and bad debt', personal financial blueprints, and the difference between the home-owner's and investor's mind-set. Above all, they've learned why it's so important to *understand* what's involved, even if they then decide to put the whole thing in the hands of an investment company.

Now, one of the first things Coach taught them were the six rules of property investing. However, these relate to the entire investment cycle, and by the end of the last session they have only got as far as actually buying a property. It's in the *next* sessions that they'll start to learn about managing their portfolio and looking after tenants.

So, let's pause and make sure we're up to speed and in the same place. And as we go quickly through the main points, why not make a note of anything you're not sure about? You can then go back over that section, or bring it up when you go to networking events or speak to a property advisor.

When looking for property:
- Look for motivated sellers;
- Get an accurate independent valuation;
- Make sure you can get a good discount; and
- Remember to check its rental potential before buying.

You can use expert help to find properties or to assess them before buying.

When you buy the property:
- Have your key team in place and ready to act fast;
- Work *with* the vendor, understanding their pressures to sell; and
- Have some negotiation techniques ready to 'seal the deal'.

When you're financing the property, your aims include:
- Maximum leverage;
- Minimal personal finance in the deal;

And remember:
- There are several ways to raise the 25% deposit; and
- As the value goes up, refinance – it's your income!

Many people use £30,000 as a benchmark target for their annual income. This can be achieved with £1million worth of property growing in value at 4% – and as we saw earlier, this means a portfolio of seven to eight properties.

So, investing in property is a serious business, not a hobby – but with the full range of professional help, investors can be as hands- on or hands-off as they like. Steve and Carol *could* just go out now and start buying properties, but Coach has lots more to teach them. They don't have to do it all themselves, but they must still become experts. They must also be 100% sure of their motivation, as must you. So take another quick look at these two graphs from chapter 2; remind yourself why property is such a good investment for anyone who wants financial freedom.

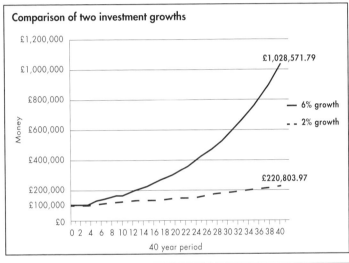

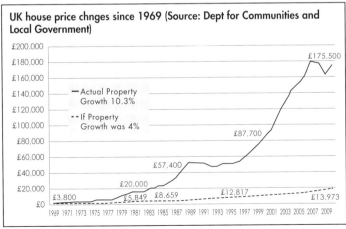

11. Refurbishing your properties

- **The Refurbishment Team**
- **Rating your team's reliability**
- **Standards – compulsory and optional**
- **Extra help**

Coach had set some interesting homework for this session, and he knew exactly what he was doing. One task was to construct a financial model involving six hypothetical purchases over a two year period. He'd asked Steve to do this, knowing he needed a little more hands-on practice with the financing concept. And then he'd asked Carol to collect names of tradespeople, including ones that had worked for them in the past. Coach still remembered their first session, when Carol was on the verge of buying completely the wrong houses. He wanted to see how much *she* had now learned about the investor mind-set. He had high hopes for both of them and was looking forward to hearing them report back.

Steve was the first into Coach's office and without a word calmly placed a green folder on the desk. It was marked 'S&C Investment Projections, 2012-2014'. Coach opened the cover, glanced through the contents page and nodded approvingly.

"I knew it!" Carol gasped, having run up the two flights of stairs to Coach's office. "You're like teacher's pet, you big softie!" She punched Steve playfully. Then, rustling through her bag, she coyly produced a rather tatty collection of stapled paper and tried to push out the creases.

"Sorry, our kids were playing in the conservatory with the dog and – well, my notes got caught up in the middle."

Coach smiled. "Hey, no worries! It's what's written on them that matters, not what they look like."

Then, noticing Steve looking downcast, Coach continued.

"Except for business plans of course. This is the kind of thing you'll be showing the bank and the mortgage companies – it pays to look professional, and this looks great. If you don't mind though, I'll take a look at this during the break in today's session. I want to push on for now – it was tough going last time so I thought today we'd take reward ourselves by talking about décor and colour schemes."

Carol tutted playfully.

"Oh I see! So that's why I've been annoying all my friends, quizzing them about plumbers and builders?"

The Refurbishment Team

Coach pushed his chair back a little to make himself more comfortable.

"Now, you've got – what is it, three children? And, so I've just learned, a dog? In that case you know how much abuse a house can – and can't – take. And as you grow your portfolio, you'll be multiplying this factor with each new purchase. So you'll need the people on your list, Carol, and as you know, they don't come cheap."

"You can say that again!" Steve chipped in. "Carol was pulling out receipts from the past couple of years, trying to find the name of some plumber we'd used, and I decided to add up the bills. I couldn't believe how much we'd spent on the house."

"Well, to be fair Steve, I did suggest you get a couple of mates to help so we could do the new kitchen ourselves, but you insisted on getting that company in."

"And look what a great job they did! But yes, I guess you're right. Maybe we should go to night-school and learn some basics. We'd save a load of money."

"Ahem …" Coach coughed politely to interrupt them. "Can I remind you both of something you said the first time we met?"

Steve and Carol looked at him, anticipating a ticking-off.

"If you could see your faces!" Coach laughed. "Anyway, I remember it word for word – you said 'You've no idea how much the business runs our lives at the moment'. Remember?"

They nodded.

"So the last thing you need is to create some kind of monster that demands every minute of your spare time, yes? Good. Well, we're going to learn how to get the right team in place so that you save yourselves time. And if saving time means you have to spend a little money, that's part of the deal."

"Ah," Steve realised, "these will be the other two-thirds of our Power Team then? But surely it's a good idea to do some of the work ourselves if it saves on outgoings?"

"You'd think so wouldn't you? If you were a professional decorator rather than a printer, I'd say 'possibly'. But even if you were, if there's *another* painter you trust who charges a *lower* hourly rate, you lose less money by using that person while you're still out there working on more lucrative jobs."

Steve's fingers hovered for a moment above his calculator until he realised he could work that out in his head.

"But," Coach continued, "just as important – if not *more* so – is speed. Look at it this way; if you have tenants already in a house and something goes wrong – a dodgy plug socket needs replacing or a tap washer wears out, nothing big, just routine stuff – golden rule is to move *fast*. You don't want the tenants grumbling about a problem; if you keep them waiting for one to be resolved you can guarantee they'll find half a dozen more. And of course, if the work is big and is stopping you putting tenants in the house, you can add lost rent to the overall bill."

Pausing, Coach could see they were taking this all in and carried on.

"No, it's quite simple. Maintenance and repairs are routine parts of managing a property portfolio, and they must be done efficiently as well as cost-effectively. And *without*, as you yourselves said, adding unreasonably to your already busy lives. Hence – your team of experts."

Coach pointed to the sheaf of papers that Carol was still clutching.

"Let's see how you've done shall we?"

Carol looked quickly through her list.

"Well, I've got three electricians, two plumbers (both people we've used) and a couple of gas fitters, although I haven't yet checked if they're properly registered. Oh," she added, looking pleased, "and we've even got a gardener."

"Not bad. OK, take a look at this." Coach handed them both a list *(figure 14, p106)*.

Steve nodded at Carol's list. "And you only got *three* of these? Looks like it'll be you in detention tonight, dear!"

"Four, counting the gardener," she retorted.

"Actually, a gardener could be useful if you need to landscape or more likely just to tidy up, but Steve, don't be so hard on Carol. What she *has* done is to get more than one name for each of her categories, which is excellent. But yes, there are rather more categories than you might have realised."

Carol, who'd been studying the list, spoke up.

Hand-out 6

Refurbishment and Maintenance

Electrician	Locksmith
Plumber	Glazier
Handyman	Roofers
Energy Performance Certifier	Drains
Domestic Appliance Repair	Gardener
House clearance	Cleaner
Gas Checks	Advertising
Carpets Large	Letting Agent
Carpets Small	

figure 14

"And they all make sense when you see them like this, although what about these two – advertising and letting agent? I thought we were talking about maintenance?"

"We are. But we're also building the entire team needed to enable you to run your portfolio with minimum input, if that's what you decide to do. And when tenants move on, you need experts ready to find you some replacements."

"True," Carol agreed. "I must say, the idea of a team that covers everything is growing on me, but I am worried about the cost. Especially as we need people we can trust, which probably means paying for premium people, hardly very good for our profit."

"Not at all. To begin with you must always get three quotes, and I've got a clever way of tracking the best ones so you never pay over the odds. I'll show you in a moment, but remember, it's all part of the investor's mind-set. Your asset is the property, and keeping it rentable is all part of paying for and protecting the asset. Look at it this way; refurb and maintenance are essential running costs, and just as you wouldn't use cowboys to repair your printing machinery, why jeopardise your assets by cutting corners? So, say you need new locks on the front door to meet insurance requirements. You don't need the same state-of-the-art alarm system you may have on your own house, but you *do* want peace of mind, so using someone you know and trust makes good sense, yes?"

Steve and Carol both looked guilty, a new alarm having been on their to-do list for nearly a year now.

"However," Coach leant forward to stress his next point, "I advise you, don't just use your own people. You might find even better options now that you're researching more thoroughly, *and* now that you can talk to other investors and get new recommendations. And," he paused and looked at them both, "I'll now show you my wonderful system for keeping tabs on who provides the best service. Carol, did you bring your laptop tonight?"

Rating your team's reliability

Delving into her bag once more, Carol pulled out a sleek black laptop, opened the lid and switched it on. Within seconds, the familiar Windows tune rang out, announcing it was ready to play.

"OK – now the name of the game is 'trust' – you need to be able to trust your workers to deliver on time and on cost. Ideally you will eventually have your core team doing all your jobs, but to start with you'll have several candidates for these top positions. So how are you going to rate them?"

Steve raised his hand. "Give them some tests? I mean, you don't want them mucking up a real house do you?"

"That's a bit daft," Carol interjected, "what are you going to test them on? Certainly not *our* house!"

Coach interrupted their banter. "The last thing you should do is announce you're trying them out – they'll simply pull out all the stops to impress. No, you need reliable people you can trust time and time again. And you need this so much that it really is worth putting in the effort early on."

He smiled at Carol. "I'm going to let you both wear your home-owners' hats, just for a moment, and answer this question. If you need some new double glazing, what do you do?"

"That's easy," answered Steve, "ask around and get some quotes."

"Precisely, and you do exactly the same at first with your portfolio properties. Carol, just pop this USB stick in would you? And then open the file called 'Traffic Lights work record demo'."

Carol did as asked, and opened the file.

As they waited for the file to load, Coach explained the background. "Ultimately you want to have a team of trusted people you use routinely, and just occasionally you'll get an additional quote from other people to check that the price is still competitive. But *until* you have that team in place, this is a great way to keep a record of who you've used and how good the work was."

The screen now displayed a spreadsheet, brightly colour-ed…." in red, amber and green *(figure 15)*.

"You can see why it's called 'Traffic Lights'! The colours are an easy way of rating individual workers. At the beginning, everyone is a red, an unknown, untested in both quality of work and cost. Obviously they've been recommended, but you are still testing them yourself.

"OK," he continued, "so what we're looking at shows how we've tracked the history of Plumber A. You can see how we keep a record of every job, and rate him red for the first three and then gradually work him up to green."

They studied the spreadsheet carefully.

Demonstration Work Record – Plumber A (four properties)

	A	B	C	C	E	F
	Job no.	Date of Job	No of other quotes obtained	Outcome	Rating after the job	
1	1	Feb 2010	2	Good	Red	
2	2	April 2010	2	Good	Red	
3	3	May 2010	2	Good	Amber	
4	4	May 2010	1	Good	Amber	
5	5	Sept 2010	1	Good	Green	
6	6	Sept 2010	1	Good	Green	
7	7	Nov 2010	0	Good	Green	
8	8	Dec 2010	0	Good	Green	
9	9	Jan 2011	0	Poor	Amber	
10	10	Feb 2011	1	Good	Amber	
11	11	Feb 2011	1	Good	Green	
12	12	March 2011	0	Good	Green	

figure 15

"If you follow the three columns on the right you can see how performance affects the number of quotes we get and the colour rating we use. As we grow more confident about Plumber A, we get fewer quotes and, eventually, we don't get any at all – see down there, November 2010, when he's been rated green for the last two jobs?"

They both nodded, absorbed by the information on the screen.

"But," said Coach, getting excited by his demonstration, "look what happened in January 2011!"

"He does a duff job by the looks of things!" Steve said.

"Quite. So he goes back to amber and look, for the next job we make sure we get another quote, just in case. But it turns out to be a blip – by February he's back to his usual high standards and so eventually we put him up to green again, and forget about other quotes."

"It's really neat, isn't it Carol?" Steve remarked.

"Yes," she agreed, "although I think I'd probably get the occasional other quote even for a long-term green – you know, just to check the price is still competitive."

"Excellent idea – and exactly what I do too!" Coach enthused.

"So in a way, the traffic light system is our own quality control device?" Steve asked.

"Exactly," Coached smiled. "And we link our records to a spread-sheet which combines all our plumbers on one sheet, all the electricians on another and so on – so we can see at a glance who is performing well. But as well as keeping these records, the really clever approach is to have someone else keeping tabs on everyone – someone you trust completely. Any ideas?"

They both scanned through the refurbishment list he'd given out earlier and each pointed simultaneously to the same word.

"Good – your handyman. He (or she!) will be your best friend, your front-line infantry and your trouble shooter – whatever description you want to use. Most little problems can be solved by the handyman, and certainly he should be the first person you send to assess a problem."

"We've got someone like that at the printing unit – amazing guy – he can mend virtually anything!"

"There you are then. And in fact, once you trust yours, you can save yourself so much time; you just let him know of the reported problem and address, and leave it to *him* to make the appointment with the tenant, and get back to you with recommendations. And there's one other role for a trusted handyman, that of 'team leader'. As long as he gets on well with people, it's worth paying him a little extra to project-manage any work that involves several people. What is it Carol? You're smiling."

"Oh sorry – I was just beginning to get a vision of us sitting at home like Chief Executives, with all these people at our beck and call."

Coach laughed. "Well, in the overall scheme of things, these costs are tiny compared to the income you're planning to generate, so it's money well spent. And to be honest, if you buy standard 3-4 bedroom town centre properties and ex-council houses, there really isn't that much maintenance, just a few jobs a year. But sure, if you like the idea of running a crack team, well good for you, why not? "

Steve winked at Carol. "I always said you'd make a good Executive's wife; didn't realise you wanted to be the Executive!" He leaned away to avoid her second friendly punch of the session.

Standards – compulsory and optional

"OK, OK – back to business." Coach summoned their attention. "Carol, you mentioned registered gas fitters earlier, remember?

It's something I want to touch on. Now, as landlords you'll need to meet certain legal requirements, so you must hire people who are qualified to do this. The last thing you want is for new tenants to go in and immediately demand this and that gets checked. Here's a list – take a look." *(figure 16)*

Hand-out 7

Standards for landlords		
Gas safety check	**Compulsory**	Required annually and must be performed by a qualified gas engineer who supplies the tenant with a certificate (cost about £75)
Electrical check	**Optional**	Recommended every five years (very few fuse boards are up to current standards)
Smoke alarms	**Unclear**	Different councils give different advice but no one wants anyone to get harmed. Strongly recommended to protect both tenants and landlords
Energy Performance Certificate (EPC)	**Compulsory**	Cost about £65 and certificate is valid for 10 years (if the house is currently tenanted, the EPC is only required when the house is vacated and a new tenant moves in)

figure 16

As they looked quickly down the page, Coach continued. "So, these are the compulsory standards you must meet and the optional ones we also recommend, but," and he winked at Carol, "there's one standard you might actually need to drop. Any idea what?"

"Mea culpa yet again!" Carol sighed.

Steve looked at her puzzled.

"Those houses I found, remember?"

"That's right," Coach added, "the ones you were naturally drawn to because they were like your own. So, you know what I'm going to say next?"

"Don't bother with marble floors and gold taps?" Steve suggested.

"Exactly. We've been talking about getting good quality, reliable workers, but please remember you are preparing and maintaining houses to let out. A good, basic finish is fine, functional not aesthetic – after all, it's a sad fact that at some point you are bound to have a house trashed. I'm afraid it does happen."

"They'll be out on their ears if it does!" Steve protested.

"They were probably being chucked out anyway – that's often the trigger," Coach explained.

Carol put her hand up. It amused Coach whenever they reverted to polite school customs.

"That's reminded me of a question I had earlier. What do we do if tenants want to decorate the place themselves? Do we say no they can't?"

"You have to make a sensible decision based on the tenants. If they're going to paint the bedrooms pitch black, and you'll be paying through the nose to get it back to magnolia when they leave, then say 'no'. But if their ideas are reasonable and don't involve removing any fittings, why not?"

"Write this down Carol," Steve laughed, "memo – remember to find tenants who are skilled DIY fanatics!"

"Actually, all you really need are tenants who regard your property as their own home," Coach said. "*They* are the ones who are likely to fix little things here and there without bothering you. And they're more likely to stay a lot longer too."

Extra help

Coach checked his own list on the desk to see what they'd not yet covered. Steve was beginning to fidget and looked rather obviously at his watch, and Coach realised they were long overdue for a coffee break.

"Sorry, I'm overrunning. We'll take a break in a minute. Just one more point to cover concerning your ace refurb team. Once you have people you trust, it's not a bad idea to get them involved *before* you buy a property, when you go to view it, and certainly if you reckon the house will need a lot of work. You'll have to pay for their time, but if it helps you fine-tune your calculations accurately, it could save you a lot of money, particularly in the form of lost rent."

"How do you mean?" Carol asked.

"Well, I like to work on the basis that with the right team in place, most properties can be refurbished within two to three weeks, no longer. And this includes things like new kitchens and bathrooms. And this really matters because you want tenants in there as soon as possible don't you? So get the expert eye to assess your *proposed* purchase for costings and time, and factor this into your offer – or even your decision to buy or not."

Coach saw that they were both flagging now.

"Right – no more! Let's have some coffee and then we'll look at the final step to get you going – finding tenants."

12. Finding the right tenants

- **DSS/LHA**
- **Advertising**
- **Bulk viewing**
- **Referencing**

"A bird in the hand is worth more than two in the bush," Coach announced as they all sat back down after their short break, "*except*, that is, in the world of tenanting."

Steve and Carol looked at him curiously, wondering if he'd overdosed on coffee during the break.

"Confused?" He smiled at them both. "It's quite simple. When you don't yet have tenants, the more applicants you have queuing up, the better. On the other hand, when you do have a bird in your hand, you want to look after it well."

They still said nothing.

"OK, what I'm really getting at is this. You're in property investing in order to make your big profit from the bricks and mortar, not from rent, right? Well, unfortunately this doesn't mean you can get away with only paying lip service to the tenanting side.

"Steve," he continued, "you've got a couple of vans, am I right?"

"Yes, for deliveries mostly. Why?"

"Well, your profit comes from printing, but the vans are crucial to being able to operate, yes? And if you don't look after them they'll soon look grubby, break down, damage your reputation and your business, and lead to reduced profit. And it's just the same with your tenanting – getting tenants in, looking after them, helping them to look after the house, keeping the properties in good condition, getting them back up and running when there's been a vacancy."

"Wow, and you say this won't take over our lives!" Carol was concerned, but Coach laughed.

"Don't worry – if you do it properly it should run smoothly and not take up much time, and you can choose to pay an agency to do as much of it as you like."

Carol didn't look convinced but Coach wasn't put off.

"Let's start with this." He handed them both a piece of paper *(figure 17)*. "This is everything we need to cover, but it's organised logically in the order you would expect to do things. It'll be a useful checklist when you're putting your first houses out for tenancy. Now, take a look at the first four items."

Hand-out 8

Setting up and running efficient tenancies

Setting up tenancies	DSS/LHA Advertising Bulk viewing Referencing Agreements and other documentation Deposits
Running tenancies	Managing tenancies 3 worst-case scenarios Insurance Rent reviews

figure 17

DSS / LHA

Steve was studying the list, and had a question.

"If this is a sequential list of what we need to do, surely 'advertising' should be the first item, not the second?"

"Good point, but no," Coach replied. "I want you to think about *who* you are advertising to before you actually do it. And if you've been talking to other investors, you may have been warned off one particular group of tenants, those getting housing benefit."

"Actually, "Carol interrupted, "we found out that many professional landlords do include DSS tenants in their portfolio. Steve's not keen though."

"Well," Coach replied, "you can have very good DSS tenants as long as you handle everything carefully, as we'll see while we work through the list. By the way we should really be referring to them as housing benefit tenants not DSS. Steve, I usually ask sceptical people this; if you had to choose between, say, someone in risky employment, or a low- or no-income housing benefit tenant, who would you go for?"

"What do you mean, 'risky employment'?" Steve asked.

"Well, perhaps working in a factory that routinely hires casual workers, or doing seasonal work at the seaside – employed now but with no real job security."

"I don't know," Steve pondered, "at least the first one's trying to earn a living."

"You can't assume the unemployed person isn't!" Carol burst in.

"Yes, but *some* rent's better than none!" Steve protested.

"Ah yes," Coach added, "but *full* rent is best of all, which is precisely why the housing benefit applicant could be the better bet. With the council paying the rent, it doesn't matter what the tenant is earning, you should still get your money. Whereas with your seasonal worker, you could be facing repeated months of excuses instead of hard cash."

Steve nodded, seeing Coach's point.

"Now, in the past you could get DSS rent direct from the council, but with the new system the Local Housing Authority (LHA) gives the housing benefit to the tenants. It helps them learn how to manage their money, to be more responsible. But there are ways around this."

They both looked up eagerly, wanting to find out more.

"I'll share a couple of company tips with you. First, charge rent *in advance*. The rules at the moment state that if your tenant is in arrears, once you're owed eight weeks' worth of rent you can apply to receive the rent direct from the council yourself. Now, we charge our rent *in advance*. So, if the tenant is defaulting, they only need to be actually in the house for about thirty days before the eight week rule kicks in."

Looking impressed, Carol was busily scribbling notes in her file.

"The other tip – write on the top of the tenancy agreement that the tenancy is granted only if the housing benefit is paid directly to you, not to the tenant. And get the *tenant* to badger the council to do this. We do this and it works for nearly 80% of tenancies.

"It's all a question of well thought through management – we'll cover it later when we look at deposits, but if you type 'LHA rent' into Google, you'll find the latest rules. You should also find the networking groups will have speakers talking specifically about LHA tenancies. As always, there are experts out there – use them!"

While Carol wrote this down, Steve asked another question.

"So can we be confident that a DSS – sorry, LHA tenant will be getting enough money to pay our rent?"

"Not automatically, no. You need to understand the 'bedroom calculator'."

"The what?"

Coached laughed. "Yes, an intriguing name, but it refers to the way a tenant's housing benefit is assessed, based on the number of bedrooms the tenant and family need. Again, you can Google for information, but in essence there are rules about how many bedrooms a tenant-plus-family needs. For example, two same-sex children can share a room, but a boy and girl, once over eleven years old, need separate rooms."

Carol had given up writing, instead making a mental note to research some websites.

"And many tenants won't understand what they can get, so it pays to be able to cross-check their entitlement yourself."

Steve was frowning, finding the whole DSS option less and less enticing. Coach realised this.

"Please remember, you'll get dodgy tenants from all walks of life. If you make sensible checks first, there's no reason to exclude DSS."

"Quite," Carol added to prevent further objections from Steve.

"One thing to remember – private landlords typically base their rent on the Local Housing Authority rents, but then *add* a small additional sum, say £20. Most people on housing benefit will also be getting tax credits, child benefits and so on, so an extra £5 a week is easily affordable. The LHA figures are a reliable reflection of the local market, being based typically on the 30th percentile of rents in the area. But the other way to test rents is by advertising – the next thing on our list I think?"

Advertising

Carol nodded towards Steve, explaining, "This is Steve's area; he's in charge of the business advertising."

"OK, that's good; now, in an earlier session we talked about advertising the property *before* you actually buy it, to test the rental demand, yes? Well I don't want to go over that point again today, but let's just think a bit about the advertisement itself. Where's the best place to advertise do you think?"

"Well, the local paper has a property section I think, once a week?"

"Great," Coach smiled back at Steve. "And if you prefer to place the advert over several days, you'll know from your business that it pays to buy in bulk, so see if you can negotiate four days for the price of three. If you're basing your buying decision on this feedback, you need to be confident you've advertised it well enough. Now, have you got that example newspaper advertisement anywhere to hand?"

Carol rifled through her file and found it.

"Good. This shows you how simple your advert should be, just the basic information."

Houses/rooms to let section

3-bed semi, Every St, Somewhere. DG, GCH, £125/wk, bonds & refs required. Tel Steph on 01234 567890

"DG? What's that?" Steve asked.

"Double glazing," Carol chided, "and the other's gas central heating. Haven't you been looking at the property details I've been collecting from estate agents?"

"OK. Still, the advert doesn't exactly sell it, does it?" Steve pointed out.

"Ah, but it's all you need," Coach explained, "especially as you don't actually own the house yet! Let me just explain it. If there was a particularly large garden, or a conservatory, you could mention that but otherwise it is deliberately simple, just the number of rooms, some basic info and the street name. Notice we haven't excluded DSS, and haven't said how much the bond is – these are things you can discuss with people once you're ready to let the house. We've also put the rent as a weekly figure—"

"Yes, I like that," Steve said, "people always multiply weekly costs by four, so it looks cheaper than putting it as a calendar monthly rate."

"That's right," Coach agreed. "Now, you could also use the internet of course. It's amazing – nowadays you just have to input the information once and you can get it listed on multiple sites like Rightmove, Zoopla and Findahouse[10]. I think it costs about £40, maybe less, and you get really good coverage."

Carol chipped in, confused once again. "Sorry, but if we advertise to test the rental viability of a property, are you saying we then advertise all over again once we've bought the property?"

"No, no, not at all. You should only have to advertise the one time, and if you get good response you just explain that the house won't be ready for six weeks or so, and offer

....
10 Chapter 20, Useful resources

to phone them back when it is. Chances are they'll still be waiting for a house, so when you're ready, you've got your tenants. And if not, you will only have bought the house if you got good rental interest, so finding a replacement won't be difficult.

"Of course," he added, "somewhere down the line you'll need to advertise for new tenants when current ones leave – and you use exactly the same method."

"I've just had a thought," Carol announced. "If we get it right and have loads of interest, we'll spend hours and hours doing viewings! Another reason I suppose to use an agent."

Bulk viewings

"Yes and no," Coach replied, "yes, a good task for an agent, but no, it needn't take up lots of time if you do it yourself. The secret is to arrange what I call 'bulk viewing'."

"Sounds uncomfortable!" Steve joked.

"It's very simple – and effective, cutting down on your time and creating a useful sense of competition. Once people start calling in response to the advert, I arrange a viewing – say, Friday at 2.00pm. I then give everyone a simple 2-page application form to fill in while they're there if they're still interested. And I can tell you, once one person starts filling in the form, they all get the itch and that's how competition grows."

"Hang on a minute," Steve said, "isn't it going to be a bit crowded?"

"Well, obviously if there are lots of viewers, stagger them – 2.00 and 2.20 – but you don't want to be there more than an hour. And if they're all together, you're more likely to notice the ones that look ideal – and the ones who don't!"

"I like the idea of this," Carol beamed, "it all sounds pretty manageable and organised."

Referencing

Coach smiled back. "Good, I'm pleased. Now, there's one last thing to do before you can make your choice of tenant – referencing. You can do this yourself, or you can pay a company that specialises in it. Whatever you do, you must be completely thorough."

"Oh, I don't think we'd ever accept a tenant who didn't have rock-solid references!" Carol said.

"Well, interesting you say that. I reckon most of the people in my company work 70% on their instinct and 30% on evidence – no, I'm not joking. You should always get references, but when you've been at it for as long as we have, you develop a kind of nose for a good tenant – and for a bad one!"

Carol looked dubious.

"It's true," Coach assured her, "but it's best to follow a strict procedure when you're starting out. And the good thing is that as you've generated high demand and competition amongst the applicants, don't be afraid to ask for wage slips and bank statements. If they don't want to show these there's probably a problem, particularly if they claim to be in employment. You can tell a lot from a bank statement!"

Carol was busy writing this all down. "Carol, sorry I should have said, I've got a handout for referencing." He looked under a few papers on the desk and, locating the right one, handed over a couple of copies *(figure 18)*.

Hand-out 9	
Referencing	
Financial	Bank statements Pay slips
Current status	Phone employer Phone landlord
Personal impression	Visit current home to assess style of living
Reasons for moving	Look for reasonable degree of stability and/or acceptable reasons for moving

figure 18

"So, you've done the financial check. The next check is with their current employer. Just give them a ring, make sure the story is correct. And do the same with the current landlord too."

"It says 'Personal impressions' here," Steve said, referring to his copy of the list, "I didn't realise we were actually supposed to *like* our tenants."

"No," Coach laughed, "but you do need to like the way they look after their home because soon it'll be *your* house they're in. What I try to do is make a surprise visit. I call them, saying I happen to be in the area, can be there in two minutes and just want to talk through something in the agreement. It may seem sneaky, but they won't have time to tidy up so you'll get a very good idea of the way they live, and how they'll treat your house.

"And finally, it's a really good idea to be a little bit nosey about why they're moving."

"The whole thing seems a bit intrusive," Carol suggested.

"I suppose it does, but you're protecting your assets remember. You need the best tenant you can get in your property, and that's all there is to it. So I'm afraid it does mean asking some questions."

"Yes, I can see that," Carol agreed. "I guess we'll get used to it."

"Oh don't worry, I've no problems being nosey," Steve chipped in. "I don't want anyone trashing my house, thanks very much."

"Actually," Coach interrupted, "asking why they're moving is less to do with risk to the house and more to do with how long they're likely to stay. What you're looking for is a good tenant who's going to stay around. So ask why they're moving in a hurry, find out if they've got problems at home, or seem to be constantly on the move. Often there are perfectly innocent reasons – relationships falling apart or needing to be closer to an elderly relative, that kind of thing. But it pays to find out."

"Of course, you can rely on traditional referencing, and as I said, pay experts to do it for you. And to be honest, it's not a lot to pay for protecting £6,000 worth of rent!"

"I think we'd want to do that, don't you Steve?" He frowned, undecided.

"A good company will check with previous landlords, current or previous employers, and will do a credit check. However," Coach looked over his glasses at them, "credit checks are not as comprehensive as you might think. It's better to get the person to run their own Experian check[11]. It's very cheap, you

....

11   See chapter 20; Useful Resources

could even get them to do it while you are there with them, and it will show things like county court judgements as well."

"But they won't do the surprise visits, will they? And I like the idea of developing a 'nose' for a good tenant." Steve was clearly more into a hands-on approach than Carol.

"Well," Coach replied, "maybe it's something you could take responsibility for Steve? Anyway, it's definitely something for the two of you to talk about. Referencing is really important, and it's also the very last step in setting up the tenancy. Once you've done that, you're straight into *managing* the tenancy, which is exactly what we're going to cover next. But first, let's take another quick break – I need to stretch my legs!"

13. Managing tenancies

- **Agreements and other documentation**
- **Deposits**
- **Managing tenancies**
- **Three worst-case scenarios**
- **Insurance**
- **Rent reviews**

As he settled himself back into his desk chair after some light stretching, Coach realised this was turning into a marathon session. He decided it was a good time to remind Steve and Carol that they could save themselves a lot of time and hassle by using professional help.

"Before we launch into looking after tenants, it seems a good time to point out the benefits of using a letting agency."

Steve looked at Carol, anticipating resistance to the idea of paying out even more money. But she was obviously waiting to see what Coach would suggest, so he carried on.

"OK – well, you *can* do all the little chores that need doing but I think it's a false economy. A typical agency will charge you 10% of the rent as their fee – so for a £500pcm house, that's £600 a year. And for that you get better tenants, fewer headaches *and* time to go looking at new properties to add to your portfolio. Remember, you're running your own business and time is precious; use what little you have for the profitable stuff, growing your portfolio."

Coach took their silence as at least partial agreement. But then, suddenly, he pushed his chair back and stood up, gripping his leg.

"Ouch – cramp! Damn circulation. I just knew it was coming on. It'll be fine in a moment – you don't mind if I walk around while talking?"

Agreements and other documentation

"Of course, there are good agencies and bad ones," Coach continued, limping around the room, "and you need to know how it all works so you can pick the right one. Now, if we can look at that hand-out from earlier, we're going to work through the second half of the list – 'agreements' through to 'rent reviews'." He waited for them to pull out the list *(figure 17)* before continuing.

Hand-out 8	
Setting up and running efficient tenancies	
Setting up tenancies	DSS/LHA Advertising Bulk viewing Referencing Agreements and other documentation Deposits
Running tenancies	Managing tenancies 3 worst-case scenarios Insurance Rent reviews

figure 17

"Right, let's assume you're now ready to sign up your tenant. You'll feel like celebrating, but it's time for some serious paperwork."

Seeing Steve grimace, Coach reassured him.

"It's just the tenancy agreement, but it's as important as any other business or legal agreement."

Carol stopped writing. "So should we use a lawyer?"

"And lose all our profit?" Steve said. "You must be joking!"

Coach chuckled, sitting down again, his cramp having eased. "Oh, you don't need to pay that kind of money," he reassured them. "For a small annual fee you can become a member of an online service for landlords and then have access to the latest documentation. For example, there's PIMS – that's Property Information Made Simple, not the drink - but you'll find others in the Useful References[12] lists that I'll be giving you. You'll see some of them let you download tenancy agreements free of charge; just be sure the site is trustworthy and if in doubt ask a more experienced investor.

"And that wraps up the paperwork; you see, it wasn't that bad!" He grinned at them both. "But next we do need to tackle the rules and regulations for landlords."

Both Carol and Steve were really beginning to flag now, so Coach decided to offer some encouragement.

"You know," he began, "I should really put all this tenancy information into a single pack, a kind of reference tool or reminder. Because like I said, once you've gone through each stage a couple of times, it really does become a relatively simple process. Even the unexpected hiccoughs become easy to deal with."

"Tell you what," Carol smiled, "I'll sell you my notes when they're finished if you like."

They all laughed.

....

12   See chapter 20: Useful resources.

Deposits

"OK – deposits. There are *two* things you need to know about deposits – how much, and what to do with them. Starting with the first, what do you reckon is a fair deposit to ask? Any ideas?"

They thought for a moment. Steve spoke first.

"Well, it's there to cover damages isn't it, so it would be daft not to get a reasonable amount."

"I agree," said Carol, "maybe two months' rent?"

"Hmm —," Coach pondered, "and that's on top of the first month's rent in advance? Seems a bit steep don't you think?"

"I suppose so," Steve agreed. "OK, one month's rent as deposit and another as rent in advance?"

"Let's think for a moment about a couple of things. First, your tenants; they're not likely to be cash-rich are they? They might struggle to pull together a huge deposit and you could lose 50% of your good potential tenants. Secondly, if the deposit were there to cover damage, let's be realistic; the damage could be anything and certainly cost a lot more than even a couple of month's rent."

"And presumably we have insurance to cover that kind of cost?" Carol asked.

"Potentially, depending on who does the damage, the tenant or someone breaking in when the house is vacant. My point is that you have to balance your own protection with what tenants can afford. So what *we* do is this; we'll ask for half a month's rent as a deposit and half a month's rent in advance. Two weeks into the tenancy, we then ask for a full month's rent, so effectively we then always run a month's rent in advance. We still have half a month's deposit as security."

"But it doesn't seem much," Steve persisted. "I mean it's not just for damages is it, it's security against non-payment of rent?"

Coach shook his head. "Ah no. It *used* to be, but not now. Since 2007, all landlords must place their tenants' deposits into a protected scheme. It's there to stop rogue landlords refusing to give deposits back. And the rules state that the money goes into a dedicated account so that it can't be spent deliberately or accidentally. Then when the tenancy ends, you inform the scheme of any damage to the property which you and the tenant agree about, and the money is divided accordingly."

"So, we're not covered against lost rent then?"

"Not with the deposit, no. But look," he added, needing to put their minds at rest, "I get clients who get incredibly stressed when a property is vacant for just three weeks, and it's crazy. Your whole cash flow model is devised to allow for short gaps between tenants, and if you've followed all the rules and got the right property and the right tenants, then vacancies or lost rent shouldn't cut into your rental income by more than, say, 5% a year. And your £50-plus positive cash flow should comfortably cover that."

They both looked relieved and reassured.

"Hey, don't forget everything else we're learning," Coach smiled at them. "If you build a big portfolio, it is almost inevitable that something *will* go wrong at some point, but I promise you, it will not become a nightmare if you stick to the rules. And in fact," he consulted the list on the desk, "that's exactly what we're going to cover now – the routine management of the operation."

Managing tenancies

Coach knew he'd been working them hard and didn't want to jeopardise their enthusiasm. So, he kept it as simple as he could.

"Basically, any problems will either be with the tenant or with the property. Tenant problems might be things like late rent, complaints from neighbours and so on, and for this you'll find that standard procedures and documents like letters of notice are all readily available – remember the PIMS website? However," and he smiled encouragingly at them both, "we find that the best approach to a problem is to talk sensibly, face to face. Most tenants don't want hassle any more than you do. Some landlords dive straight in, ranting and raging at them, and wonder why they don't get any cooperation! It might be a very small problem, easy to fix, and once you get talking you can actually help the tenant to sort it out. Don't be afraid to go round and approach it calmly."

Steve and Carol both nodded their agreement.

"One tip," Coach added, "is to text on the mobile rather than calling, just to make arrangements to meet. If someone's short of money, they'll appreciate not having to use up their phone credit."

Carol couldn't help noticing how Coach's soft side occasionally showed through.

"Bottom line," Coach said, "is that if you rent out a house for ten years, you must expect to have a few months in total when tenants don't pay, for whatever reason. It's just the way it works, and it's all accounted for in the numbers, so just accept it."

"To be honest," Steve spoke up, "I'm far more worried about problems with the houses than with the tenants."

"Which is what I'm coming on to now. Remember when we talked about your refurb and maintenance team? Well, if you've got them in place, what's there to worry about?"

"The cost?" Steve suggested.

"Not if you've got your good positive cash flow. Rent coming in, minus insurance, maintenance and so on, leaving a £50-plus surplus, remember? Well most months you probably won't actually be spending the monthly maintenance component, so there'll probably be a really healthy sum here by the time you do need it. The only thing you should be thinking about is your time. Do you want tenants ringing at 11 pm to say the tap's dripping? Of course not, and neither will your plumber. So you need simple, clear guidelines for your tenants, when they can and can't ring, what constitutes an emergency, that kind of thing."

Carol stopped writing.

"So what *does* constitute an emergency?"

"I think you must use your common sense – what would be an emergency in your own home?"

"I suppose … floods, gas leaks …"

"Exactly, so show your tenant where the stop cock is – and how to use it. And for gas, obviously they must get out and call for help. It's all common sense. Just establish your boundaries – say, no phone calls after 7pm or whatever seems reasonable."

Coach was about to push on to the next topic when he suddenly remembered a useful tip.

"There is one instance when a problem becomes a definite bonus, something you asked about earlier – and that's when the tenant starts talking about redecorating."

"Now that really would be pushing their luck!" Steve objected.

"Not if they want to do it themselves," Coach replied. "I keep stressing that the more stable and secure tenants feel, the more likely they are to look after the house – and *not* to bother you with every little problem which they're more than capable of resolving. And they're more likely to stay for longer too. So, if they're taking pride in the place and want to freshen up the paintwork, why not?"

Steve nodded agreement, seeing the wisdom in Coach's argument.

Three worst-case scenarios

"Of course …" Coach felt they were sufficiently reassured now to contemplate the worst that might happen, "you *may* have to play tough on occasions. I guess the three most common scenarios are removing a tenant who won't pay rent, dealing with a tenant who's trashed the house, and having the house ransacked whilst it's empty between tenants. Let me just touch on each of these in order.

"So, your tenant refuses to pay, or perhaps is repeatedly treating the property badly, and you want them out. Quite right too! Unfortunately, the worst tenants often know how to play the system, and even if you do everything right it can sometimes take up to four months to get them out."

Steve breathed in sharply.

"But," Coach continued, "with your contingency fund, say £3,000 for a portfolio of five houses, you can maintain the mortgages while there's no rent."

"But surely we're legally protected as well – I mean, the tenant is the one in the wrong," Carol pointed out.

"Absolutely. And it's sections 8 and 21 of the 1985 Housing Act that you need to refer to. But of course, the law is always changing, so once again, if you've signed up to a site like PIMS you'll always be able to look up whatever's the most recent version."

"OK, moving on to the second scenario where the tenant has trashed the house. In a way, the problem is the same for the third scenario, damaged property, so why don't I cover these together? To be honest, even an insane or malicious tenant can only do so much money's worth of damage – you might need a new carpet, some replastering, but it's unlikely to cost more than, say, £3,000. If the property's been vacant and someone's broken in, they're more likely to be serious criminals and will go for things like copper and other metals, whatever they can sell. So we're talking kitchens, bathrooms, central heating – all things that might get broken."

"Will our insurance cover this?" Steve asked anxiously.

"I'm glad you asked that Steve, as it's the next item on my list."

Insurance

"And," Coach continued, "the answer is 'yes' for scenarios one and three, provided you have the right policy. It's also 'yes' for malicious damage by the tenant, but sometimes it can be hard to prove the damage wasn't just normal wear and tear. Of course, as I've just said, the damage isn't likely to add up to all that much anyway, but talking about insurance – I don't know what your personal opinion of it is but—"

"Not a very high one," said Steve, "although we did get replacement machinery a few years ago thanks to a policy we opted for when we bought it. Carol insisted on it and, of course, she was right."

Coach smiled at them both. "Good, well it's the same when you're a landlord. You can fine-tune your policy a little to suit your circumstances, but it must be a policy designed for rental properties. Once again, go to an expert who knows about these things! And make sure it covers the property when it's empty. I bet your own home policy has a clause about not covering you if the house is empty for more than thirty days or so?"

Carol nodded.

"Well, you might need longer than that if you're refurbishing or are between tenants. That would also make sure you're covered against the third scenario, damage whilst vacant. And then the other cover you *must* include is against loss of rent."

"There," interrupted Steve, "I knew insurance would cover this."

"Ah – but only if something happens to the house which prevents you renting it, not just when it happens to be empty between tenants."

"Yeah, I suppose that's asking a bit much isn't it? Otherwise you could leave it empty all year and just claim off the insurance!" Steve grinned.

"Quite, so if the house burns down or your tenant has to be rehoused temporarily because the roof blows off, you can claim back the lost rent. And I think it only adds another £1 or so to the policy each month. Overall you should expect to pay £15-20 a month per property."

"Hey Carol, imagine if there was a fire – and obviously nobody gets hurt – but the insurance covers the lost rent *and* pays for the refurbishment! Not bad!"

Coach tutted. "Steve, I think all in all you'd be happier without the fire? Just make sure you're covered, just in case."

"OK, but it doesn't seem very fair that we have to insure on behalf of the tenants' safety, but can't guarantee a pay-out if a tenant trashes the place – you know, what you said about proving it's not just wear and tear."

"Bottom line, Steve, is that if you pay the money you can insure against anything. But remember, insurance companies have to make a profit and they only do this by charging more for premiums than they pay out on claims. Much better surely to keep your contingency fund healthy rather than hand over, say, 30% of your rent to the insurers, 'just in case'?"

Steve nodded slowly in agreement.

Rent reviews

"And finally," said Coach, pushing the list to one side, "let's assume you've got *good* tenants, it's all running well; when is the time to put up the rent?"

Steve and Carol couldn't help smiling at Coach's style, always ending on a high note.

"Every year?" Steve suggested tentatively.

"Absolutely!" Coach agreed. "It must be in the tenancy agreement, in black and white, that the rent will go up each year by three to five per cent."

"Isn't that a bit of a disincentive to some potential tenants?" asked Carol.

"And," Steve interjected, "wouldn't it be better to hold the rent down if we've got good tenants?" He was clearly still contemplating all the problems they'd been discussing.

"No, definitely not." Coach was very clear on this. "If you don't put it up each year, you're just creating a big problem for the future – remember the mortgage condition? The one that requires rent to be at least 125% of the mortgage repayment? Well, because of this, when you want to remortgage, you will have to put the rent up; so you're just creating a problem if you haven't been doing it in yearly increments . Remember too that you're running a business and you've got to keep up with inflation."

"I suppose," Carol added, "as you say, as long as it's there in the basic contract, everything is fair and above board. And you're right, it *is* a business."

"And," Coach added, "even if they're new to renting, most tenants understand it when they sign the tenancy agreement, so there's no problem."

He could see his students really had reached their limits of concentration for one night. He wanted to give them some reassurance before they left.

"My last word on the subject is, once again, to remind you that you can always pay an agency to handle most of this, so please, I do *not* want you to start having nightmares or getting cold feet. Managing your portfolio as a going concern can be a pleasure when everything runs smoothly, which is a *lot* of the time."

He closed his file and declared the session over.

14. Tax and accounting

- **Tax efficiency (income, capital gains and inheritance tax)**
- **Mortgages – interest only vs repayment**
- **Minimising your tax bill**

This evening's session was a highlight for Carol as the money-minder of the business, but one that Steve had been dreading. He'd even tried to get out of it, suggesting to Coach that they'd cover much more ground if he wasn't there. Nonsense had been the reply – you're in it together. He'd then complimented Steve's work on his mind-set, pointing out how business-like his approach had now become, evidenced by his tough attitude to nuisance tenants. And so, armed as always with his calculator, Steve was now sitting in his usual chair alongside Carol, ready to face the complexities of property tax.

"Now then," beamed Coach, "one of my favourite topics – tax! And for a very good reason too. But you'll be surprised how little there is for us to talk about. Do you know why?"

They both shrugged. Steve began to feel a little less anxious about the session.

"Because I am a Property Expert, and you will soon be Professional Property Investors – but none of us are *tax* experts!"

Not for the first time, Coach reminded Carol of her favourite uncle, the retired accountant.

"Presumably a lot of this can be handled by an accountant?"

"Spot on!" Coach agreed. "Tax is one of those frustratingly elusive things to pin down, and tax law is always changing. So yes, you need an expert in place, and remember, your own accountant may be excellent for your business but might know nothing about property. You must work with experts."

"Surely *we* need to understand the basics though?" Carol asked, worried the session was about to be brought to a premature end. She took immense care and pride in managing the business accounts and was looking forward to demonstrating her knowledge.

"Yes you do – and for a very good reason; it reflects the complete beauty and simplicity of property investment as a highly efficient income generator. And the key word is 'efficient'."

Tax efficiency

Income tax

"OK," Coach began, "you remember when we talked about spreading your equity across several houses, putting in as little of your own money into each?"

They both nodded.

"Good – that was how to make your money work harder. Now I want you to be able to protect that money by maximising tax avoidance. *Avoidance*," he emphasised, seeing Steve's eyebrows go up, "not evasion! It's all perfectly legal, just reducing your tax bill. "

Steve grinned.

"First of all, as with your printing business you have a gross income – your rents – from which you deduct your running costs, and then you're left with the net or taxable income. Now, somewhere I've got a very simple overview of what you can deduct from the gross income."

Leafing through the papers on his desk, Coach found what he was looking for and handed one sheet to each of them *(figure 19)*.

Hand-out 10	
What can be off-set against tax	
The interest on the mortgage	All interest can be offset, but none of the capital
Building insurance	
Any maintenance of the property	NB this covers routine maintenance (repairing and replacing) but excludes significant work done to change or improve the property, such as an extension
Letting agency fees	

figure 19

They both scanned the list.

"You can see straight away why it helps to have a nice big interest-only mortgage!" Steve said. "It must be the largest item on this list?"

Coach was delighted to hear Steve say this. "Some property investors don't have your business background and are determined to buy a house for cash, anything rather than having debt. Remember the inheritance example – you inherit £100,000 and either buy one house for cash, or four with £25,000 equity in each. With the single house, OK, you've got no loan to repay but you don't have the mortgage interest tax relief either. With the four houses, and four lots of mortgage interest payments financed by the rent, you should have a very small tax bill. Especially," he added, pointing to their lists, "when you have factored in these other items."

"It's very neat isn't it, Steve?" Carol commented, wanting to keep Steve's enthusiasm on the boil.

"Just a minute," Steve replied. He was scribbling on some paper and punching numbers into his calculator. "Sorry, I was just trying it out." He showed Carol what he'd been writing (figure 20).

Assume £70,000 mortgage

Rent per month: £560

The interest on the mortgage @6% = £350/mth

Building insurance   £20

Any maintenance of the property   £80

Letting agency fees @10% = £56

Which leaves taxable income of £54 per month = £648 a year!

figure 20

"Look how small I've got the taxable income! And I suppose, if we had the cash, we could do some more maintenance on the house and eliminate the liability altogether?"

Looking very pleased, Coach spoke again.

"And with our investment model based on leverage, it's self-perpetuating too. Each time you remortgage you increase the interest payments, which counteracts the annual rise in the rent you're charging."

"Net result, minimum income tax," Carol declared confidently.

"Hang on a minute," Steve interrupted. "You said mortgage interest payments, but what about the capital? Surely it depends on what type of mortgage we have?"

"Indeed it does, and we'll take a look at that in a moment. The important thing for now is to understand that it all comes down to efficient business accounting, and as people running a business, it's nothing new for you two."

"You're right there!" Steve laughed. "Carol's always banging on about reducing tax liabilities."

"Well it's the same thing," she retorted. Then, turning to Coach for back-up, she added "isn't it?"

"It is. But of course, income tax isn't the only type of tax we need to think about."

Capital gains tax

"Let's go back to the investor who's *not* business-minded. Let's say I've convinced them to buy four houses with mortgages, and after several years they've added another four. All looking good – until I hear that they plan to sell the first four and use the profit to pay off the mortgages on the other four, leaving them fully paid up and bringing in a nice rent."

"Well, that's daft isn't it?" Steve said, "They'll be paying income tax on the rent for the rest of their lives."

"I wouldn't say daft," Coach said, "remember, some people will always feel happier with less debt, even if it's good debt. But they're also now exposed to another type of tax – capital gains. In other words, tax based on the profit they made from selling the four houses."

"So it's a kind of tax double-whammy!" Steve laughed. Carol tutted, but secretly she was pleased he was so focused.

"Which is why my advice is," Coach continued, "never to sell a property. Steve, can you help out with our calculator?"

Steve sat up, fingers at the ready.

"OK – this £100,000 house we always talk about; if it doubles in value every ten years, then after *twenty* years it's worth £400,000. Let's say you then sell it, making a profit of £300,000. Well, that's your capital gain. And Steve, let's say capital gains tax is set at 22% as it is just now, that means a bill of …?"

"£66,000 – hell, that's a lot!"

"Quite. But the tax rate *used* to be 40%, so that would have been how much?"

Steve whistled and then gave the answer. "£120,000!"

"Exactly," Coach concluded. "You see, for as long as you own a property that's going up in value, you are building up a tax liability that will kick in if you ever decide to sell it. But when you die, any capital gains liability dies *with* you. It doesn't pass on to your beneficiaries along with your estate. So, in my example, if the owners were fed up with managing all eight properties, they would have saved themselves a lot of money by simply appointing someone to do this for them – certainly cheaper than handing all that cash over to the tax man! But the main problem was that they weren't using the investor mind-set – remember, good and bad debt. To them, any debt is bad, hence the urge to pay it all off."

Carol was looking thoughtful. "But surely, when we do die and pass the portfolio on to the children, there must surely be *some* tax liability that goes with it? What about inheritance tax?"

"Yes, and we want to minimise that too! Let me explain."

Inheritance tax

"To make sure your survivors don't curse you for evermore after you're dead and buried," Coach looked at them both over his glasses, "you *must* have an expert accountant who is experienced in property investment. There will certainly be a tax liability – inheritance tax – but if you plan carefully, this can also be minimised."

Carol put her hand up. "Actually, this is the *only* significant tax we have to worry about isn't it? We'll have kept income tax as low as possible, and you've explained how capital gains isn't an issue as long as we don't sell any properties. I'm beginning to see just how tax-efficient this property investment is!"

"That's right," Coach agreed, "and to minimise inheritance tax, it's just a case of balancing assets and liabilities. You see, when you die, your estate owes tax on the *net* value of your assets. Now, why not write this down on the hand-out, to keep it all in one place?"

They both sat waiting like a pair of attentive secretaries.

"OK. Firstly, there's a set amount of money you can inherit tax-free – at the moment I think it's £325,000."

Tax-free: £325,000

"So, let's say your own home is worth £300,000 and the mortgage is paid off. With a net value of £300,000, you're safely below the tax-free threshold, so nothing is owed. Right, now let's say you have seven properties, worth, oh, a million pounds."

Portfolio: £1,000,000

"Right, if the mortgages are all paid off, and you've got, say, £300,000 equity in your own house, your total value is £1,300,000. So your estate that is taxable is worth £975,000, which at 40% gives you an inheritance tax bill of?"

$$1,300,000$$
$$(325,000)$$
$$\overline{975,000}$$
$$\underline{X0.4}$$
$$390,000$$

"Wow – £390,000!" Steve revealed.

"Quite – not something you want to leave your children with! So, if instead you've done what we keep talking about and *not* paid off the mortgages, you'll have about £750,000 owing on the portfolio. We still have the £300,000 equity in the portfolio, so the total value is the same. But what happens now?"

$$1,300,000$$
$$(750,000$$
$$(325,000)$$
$$\overline{225,000}$$
$$\underline{X0.4}$$
$$90,000$$

"Still a lot!" Carol said.

"Yes, but less than a quarter of what it could have been – and look at it the other way round; instead of shelling out £750,000 repaying the mortgages, you've had that spending power for something else! But," and he laughed, "if you're not happy with that, you'll have to take it up with the Chancellor of the Exchequer."

Mortgages – interest-only *vs* repayment

"You said you'd come back to mortgages?" Steve prompted.

"Yes, you're right – well the choice is between repayment and interest-only, and personally I would always recommend the latter."

"Really?" Steve questioned. "To me it always feels a bit dangerous not to be paying off *any* of the capital, just the interest."

"Ah – but what have we just been talking about? With our model you *never* pay back the capital, that's the whole point."

"What?"

"Investor mind-set, remember?" Coach said. "Look, if it's your own home, then of course you want to pay off the mortgage, the sooner the better, so that you can enjoy the house knowing that whatever happens, it is completely paid for. But with your portfolio, we're doing the opposite. Think about it, at every opportunity we're *increasing* the mortgage, not paying it off, because that's where our income comes from."

"Yes of course." Steve nodded thoughtfully.

"And," Coach continued, "with an interest-only mortgage, you keep the repayments high enough to offset your rental income. If you were paying off the capital as well, the interest would start to go down and then your income tax liability would increase."

Minimising your tax bill

"OK, I'll now send you on your way with today's final hand-out." Coach smiled, noticing Carol's eagerness to see what it was. His clients sometimes found this tax session one of the hardest to follow, and he liked to leave them with something positive to think about. The hand-out was an illustration of just how tax-efficient a well-run property portfolio can be *(figure 21)*.

Hand-out 11

Tax-efficient portfolio management

1. *Start with a 4-house portfolio and keep re-mortgaging and releasing tax-free cash. During the 20 year period, the portfolio has generated an estimated £800,000 tax-free income and incurred no income or capital gains tax.*	**2010**
	Buy 4 houses, total worth £400k, made up of
	  £100k equity
	  £300k mortgages
	2010 -2030
	Withdraw total of £800,000 tax-free income
	Pay £0 in income tax and capital gains tax
	2030
	Total worth now £1,600k, made up of
	  £400k equity
	  £1,200k mortgages

2030
Children inherit portfolio worth £1,600k
 	
Net value:
  £1,600K
  (£1,200k) mortgages
  £400k taxable net value
At 40%: £160k tax bill
 	
Sell one house:
  £400k
  (£300k) repay mortgage
  £100k towards inheritance tax
 	
Left with:
  £1,200k portfolio, made up of
 	
  £900k mortgage
  £300k equity
	2. *Now the children inherit the portfolio.*
	
	They are liable for inheritance tax based on the net value of the portfolio. They can raise a large part of this by selling just one of the properties, leaving them with a portfolio worth £1,200k, ready to grow and provide more tax-free income.
	
	NB: this assumes that the tax-free allowance from the deceased's estate has been used up (for example, they left their own house in the will, using up the £325,000 per person inheritance tax-free allowance). If not, then the children's tax liability will be even less as this can be added into the portfolio calculations and offset against the total liability.

figure 21

15. What about the downsides?

Just before the final coaching session let's take another quick break. I want you to feel confident in property investment as a means to financial freedom. And just like Carol and Steve, you are probably wondering if there's a catch. Is it all too good to be true? Well the answer is simple. As with anything in life and certainly in business, things can and will go wrong. There will be downsides. However, if you *have a plan and stick to it*, you will be fine. You will have the money to cover emergencies and to ride out any lean times. I want you to remember that property investment income is based on average performance over time. This is its key strength. And if you have planned for the things that might go wrong, your portfolio will remain healthy long-term.

So, let's just take a quick look at the kind of things that trip up the badly-prepared investor and then you'll know how to avoid both them and the stress they bring.

Breakdowns and repairs

Think of your own house over a ten year period; things go wrong, break down or need replacing. It's just the same in your investment properties. Boilers need replacing, roofs get damaged, windows break. And this is why you have your contingency fund – remember, £3,000 for anything from one to four properties should be enough. With your positive cash-flow, of course, you will be adding to this all the time. We find that by adding £80 a month maintenance money per property to your positive cash-flow target, you should always have enough to cover these bills without having to dip into personal finances.

And of course for each month that you *don't* have a repair bill to pay, your contingency fund grows bigger.

The tenant doesn't pay

Again, this will happen at some point over a typical ten year period. And as Coach explained, it can take over four months to evict a tenant who knows how it all works. So be prepared. In addition to the contingency fund to cover rent shortfall, you can pay a small annual fee to belong to a web-based organisation (e.g. www.riky.co.uk). This will give you templates for landlord letters, and you can get free legal advice online or over the phone. So you see, you don't need to know the housing law inside out, just how to find someone who does. Then you're prepared and can deal with it when it happens.

A property won't rent

Now, if you buy according to the rules you shouldn't have this problem. But sometimes you find that a property you've had for some time becomes difficult to rent. Perhaps the area has been developed or a school has closed. Whatever the reason, if this happens you need to be prepared to reconsider the property – is it still worth keeping? It might cost a few thousand to sell but if you can replace it with one that rents out without difficulty, it's worth it in the long run. Just remember, there is no point at all in having any property in your portfolio that is not extremely easy to rent.

The market goes down and you cannot release money

Your income is based on refinancing as the property goes up in value, so this is the one downside that worries most investors most. And at the time of writing we have had three years when this has happened. But again I have to stress, this is a long-term income strategy based on average performance over a period of years. The illustrations throughout the book have shown time and time again that looking at increments of twenty or even just ten years, average performance has always been good. So what does being prepared for market dips actually mean? Well, set a realistic income target based on cautious growth. Then if you hit a particularly good year, spend what you planned to spend but bank the rest. As with your contingency fund, this surplus will cover you if the market slows down.

Trying a different type of property investment without learning first

Coach has repeated many times to Steve and Carol that their work is all to do with standard buy to let portfolios – not overseas property, HMOs, etc. But he also tells them that those are good opportunities provided you learn all about it. He's right. The fastest way to lose money in any investment is by not taking the time to learn how it all works, not learning the rules. So, if you decide you want to branch out and move into a new investment area that's fine, but do take the time to talk to experts at property clubs, find out exactly what you need to know and do – and learn the rules.

So, I hope this reassures you. Take the long-term perspective, identify your goals, make plans for reaching them and plans for when things go wrong – and stick to them. This way, whatever happens, you're prepared; and whilst it would always be nice if things just ticked over without problems, at least you will be more than ready to deal with them.

16. Other types of property investment

- **Standard UK family houses (3-4 bed town houses and ex-council)**
- **HMOs and student lets**
- **Flipping**
- **Buy to develop**
- **Buy abroad**

It was two weeks since they'd last met Coach, and tonight was their final session. The two of them reminisced as they walked from the car to Coach's office.

"Hey, I looked through the calendar this morning. Do you realise it's only ten weeks since I bumped into Phil that night at the station?"

Carol looked at her husband. "I know. And look how far we've come! We owe him a huge favour."

"I've been thinking about that," Steve said, "and I reckon we should invite him to celebrate when we buy our first property. What do you think?"

"Great idea!" Carol replied. "And let's hope that's soon. It's funny – I know exactly why those four houses I found were completely wrong and I know what to look for now – but I'm still nervous about buying the first one."

"But I hope you're excited too?" It wasn't Steve who asked this but Coach who had overheard her as she climbed the final stairs to his door. "Come in both of you! Well – our final session; how does that feel?"

"Fantastic," Steve replied, then realising how that sounded, he blushed.

"I think what Steve means is that it's been an amazing experience," Carol said, covering Steve's embarrassment. "But we've got to stop thinking about it now – and just get on and *do* it, which is a bit scary."

Coach laughed. "Being scared is good in a way. It means you know how much you have to get right if you're to make it a success. I probably shouldn't say this, but I had the tiniest doubt when we first met; you seemed to be on such different wavelengths. But since then I've been so impressed by the way you've both grown into serious investor-minded people. And you'll make a great team too."

Now Carol was blushing, so Coach announced the topic of the day – deciding what type of property to invest in.

Standard UK family houses (3-4 bed town houses and ex-council)

"OK," Coach began, "cast your minds back to the key rules of property investment. Which one will *most* help you decide what to buy?"

Steve frowned. "Well, one of the rules was simply 'Buy the right property' but that doesn't really say very much does it?"

"Surely the right one is one that will rent out easily?" Carol looked pleased with herself.

"Oh I see," Steve responded, "so we're talking about the right location, schools and so on."

"No silly – it means do we buy new-build, apartments, semi-detached, all that kind of thing."

"Precisely," Coach said, "and I can tell you that all the houses in my own portfolio are three or four bed houses, either town centre terraced or ex-council houses."

Steve frowned again. "You really think buying council houses is a good idea?"

"Definitely. Avoid the rough areas – find out where lots of council houses are now privately owned. And then what you get is a really well built house, good sized rooms, front and back gardens – ideal for families and easy to maintain as well."

"Certainly ticks a lot of boxes!" Carol said.

"And if you get it right, you'll place your 'TO RENT' advert and get thirty people interested straight away. And that's what you want isn't it Steve?"

"Yes," Steve answered, "but what about smaller places? I mean, a flat without a garden needs less maintenance and, as children are more likely to trash the place, maybe buying family houses is just asking for trouble."

"An interesting angle," Coach replied, "but while smaller properties may be easier to manage, you'll find a much faster turnover of tenants; young couples who decide to have a baby, single people getting married. Do you know, the average one or two bed property lets to a single tenant for only eighteen months? Whereas, with the right three or four bed house, you can get lucky and have the same tenants for ten, even twenty years."

"Oh I see," Steve conceded, "I suppose I'm forgetting that even though they're tenants, for some this will be their long-term home."

"And they're the ones who are most likely to look after the place, don't forget," Carol added.

Coach smiled at them both, enjoying watching them work it out for themselves.

Steve had another question.

HMOs and student lets

"What about students? Not here as we've only got one small college, but there are two university towns on the doorstep. They must provide a ready source of tenants?"

"No way!" Carol said firmly. "Think of the mess!"

Coach smiled. "You're both right in a way. If your priority is to find tenants easily, students are one way to go; but if you want to have responsible tenants who will look after the property, it could be a gamble. On the other hand, some families can be far more destructive than half a dozen students! But you've hit on something interesting – the HMO."

Steve and Carol both fell silent, each trying to guess the words behind the initials.

"Her Majesty's … er …" Steve gave up.

"House of Multiple Occupancy," Coach explained. "What it really means is any house where there are separate tenants, each paying their own rent independently, rather than a single family."

"God, that sounds messy," Carol said. "I can just imagine, the one student who never pays, who's never there when you go round to chase it up—"

"—or who *is* there, but is stoned out of his mind!" Steve laughed.

"I think you're in danger of stereotyping," Coach chastised them both. "And an HMO needn't have students. Lots of young professionals share rental houses. There's one definite advantage in multiple tenant houses – if one person leaves, you only lose a portion of the rent until you replace them, rather than having a whole house sitting there empty."

"On the other hand," Carol suggested, "they're more likely to move on more often perhaps? Once they've saved a deposit for their own house, or just if they fall out with the other tenants."

Seeing their minds wandering off in different directions, Coach coughed to summon their attention.

"HMOs may not be the ideal option for you two because you already have your hands full running the printing business. But they're still good investment options and it's important I cover the basics of HMOs so that you know. Firstly, depending on the number of tenants, the number of floors and so on, you may have to apply for a license from the local council. You'll also have to comply with their rules about emergency lighting, alarms and so on. On the other hand, it's a good way to maximise the rent from a house – you can convert the dining room and even the lounge if there's still a decent sized kitchen – turning a four bed into a six bed house."

Steve and Carol now both looked disapproving of the idea, but Coach continued.

"As landlord, you'll be responsible for council tax, utility bills, and things like broadband. And if you let to students, you need to know a few things too. Firstly, some universities are building more student accommodation, so the housing demand might be going down; it's something to check up on. Also, in many university towns, students expect to rent for only ten months of the year. Some landlords like the empty period to clean up and prepare for the next lot. But if you don't like the idea of lost rent, you need to buy in a town where student demand is so great that landlords *can* charge a full twelve months."

Coach looked down at his checklist. "Oh yes, and another thing to bear in mind – banks are not so keen to lend against HMOs, particularly when the market's down. If they have to repossess, they want it to be a simple process and with a HMO they'll find themselves acting as landlord to multiple tenants, which costs them time and money."

"Well," Steve said, "it doesn't look as though HMOs are your favourite type of investment property."

"No you're wrong," Coach corrected him, "the HMO model is in many ways ideal for someone who wants to run their portfolio as their primary business. You see, a 4-bedroom house brings in, say, £600 in rent; add another couple of rooms at £60 a week and you're looking at £1300 rent for the same property. Yes you'll have to pay the extra bills but look – they're not going to be more than £300, so you're still clearing an extra £400 rent. I actually still have a couple of HMOs in my own portfolio – I had five at one time but they are incredibly hard work."

Steve nodded thoughtfully while Coach continued.

"It's something to think about in the future. But there are still a couple more investment options to consider as well, starting with *flipping.*"

Flipping

"You'll hear about 'flipping' at networking events – and in a sense it's the complete opposite of everything we've talked about – rather than property investing, this is more like property trading. In other words you buy and then sell as fast as you can, and your profit comes from the sale."

"Ah," said Steve, "hence 'flipping'! Well, if you can do that, why bother with all the hassle of tenants?"

"Two reasons," replied Coach, "and both are to do with risk. It's a completely different financial model, short-term for a quick profit. And secondly, it can be a gamble, especially if the market is slow. The only reason I mention it is because of one of the other rules – any ideas?"

Carol put her hand up. "Buy at a discount?"

"Exactly. For as long as you're looking for properties, you'll be hunting down the big discounts, and these are the ones that you *can* in theory turn around and sell – or 'flip'. You'd have to factor in your buying costs, so a house worth £100,000, bought for £80,000 and sold for £95,000 would net you around £10,000 after buying and selling fees and mortgage costs. The clever thing is that if you buy with a mortgage, say putting down £20,000 deposit, then in effect you've generated 50% profit on your money. But you must be confident of a buoyant market and a house that will sell quickly."

"Hmm, it's not the same thing at all, is it?" Carol agreed. "We're after a long term strategy, and I don't think either of us wants to take that risk."

"Fair enough," Coach replied. "It's something you can have at the back of your mind, just in case you do stumble across an incredible bargain. But," and Coach looked over his glasses to ensure their attention, "buying to flip requires a completely different set of rules to buying to let. What they *do* have in common is that you absolutely must stick to the rules. So, before you consider flipping, you need to spend some time learning all about it first."

Steve had a question. "OK, but leaving aside the rules—"

Coach frowned at him.

"I mean, *as well as thinking* about the rules, a good property for flipping might still need a lot of work doing, which means you couldn't flip it quickly anyway surely?"

"Ah – that's a different type of purchase altogether – we can talk about that now."

Buy to develop and sell/rent

"And," Coach continued, "there are two types of projects involving renovations – buying the house to sell on, and buying it to add to your investment portfolio and let. In both cases, the essential factor is the cost of renovation. If you're going to sell it, then obviously the renovation costs will eat into your profit."

"Surely," Carol interrupted, "it's just the same if we plan to hang onto the house? The renovation cost has to come from somewhere, either our equity, or from the profit we make from refinancing."

"Exactly," Steve added, "I don't see what's different between this and just buying a portfolio property and deciding to replace the kitchen and bathroom?"

"If that's all you're doing, then not much," Coach agreed, "but we should really be talking about 'development' rather than 'renovation'. The best way to make money doing up a house for sale is to add to it – either split it into two smaller properties, or perhaps build an extension in the garden. That's where the real profit comes from. But just as with your portfolio properties, you need excellent builders who you trust, realistic quotes and timelines, and to be able to cover the buying, selling and mortgage costs until the house is not just ready, but sold."

"I see – it's not what we want is it Carol?"

"Well, no, but as Coach says, who knows – we might stumble across a property that gives an amazing opportunity and we'd be stupid to ignore it on principle."

"Steve," Coach added, "think of property development more as a joint venture project – you remember, when we talked about financing? Well, in this case, you could go into partnership with the builder who provides the expertise and labour, while you provide the finance. People do actually make good incomes this way, but as always," he peered across at them both, "the ones who succeed are experts in what they do."

"I think we should just do one thing at a time," Steve was convinced by this, "carry on learning about buy to let investments and get really good at that."

Buying abroad

"I completely agree," Coach said. "But there's one other type of purchase you'll hear about, one that follows the same model pretty closely – and that's buying property abroad."

Carol reached over and put a restraining hand on Steve's knee. They'd had an argument that week about holidays which revolved around the question of buying a holiday apartment. She knew Steve liked the idea but she realised this was not what Coach was talking about. However, Coach's mind-reading skills kicked in.

"Ah, you're thinking about somewhere exotic and hot, in the sun, a place you could use yourselves once or twice a year, yes?"

As neither would admit nor deny it he carried on.

"I quite understand, and there are some amazing bargains advertised in the papers and magazines. Certainly, your money may seem to go much further, but without even thinking about the future returns based on value increase, just think of the practicalities!"

They were both nodding agreement as they thought of exactly that – having to travel thousands of miles for an inspection, dealing with foreign builders and their different customs, language barriers, tax complications – it was a nightmare.

"No, in my opinion much better to add that project to your 'Dream Bucket' and make it an incentive to work harder at your local portfolio!"

There was a long silence, eventually broken by Steve.

"I think maybe a good, solid council house in a reasonable area is the best option after all!" Carol laughed. Coach knew now that Steve would make a very sensible investor. In fact, looking at them both he felt they were lucky to have such different but compatible outlooks. They'll go far, he thought, but they need one final push in the right direction.

"So, as you know we'll meet up in a month or so to see how it's all going, but for now I want you to do one thing for me – well, for you of course. Any idea?"

They looked up expectantly.

"I want you to take action! You're at the critical point where we've done loads of theorising but nothing for real. Oh, I know," he'd noticed Carol pulling a face, "you've started going to networking events which is excellent. And you must keep going, regularly, for a long time. Eventually you'll be giving advice to the next generation of new investors, but for now go along and talk, ask questions and learn. But no, I want you to do more than that."

Again they looked at him, waiting for their final instruction.

"You are one step away from buying your first property. Do you know what that step is?"

"Get professional help?" Carol suggested.

Coach beamed. "Spot on as usual. You already know you need a solicitor, an accountant, surveyor, handy man and so on – but the one avenue you should still explore is a professional Property Advisor. Find a good one with a good reputation and you'll have the very best help getting your portfolio off the ground."

Carol finally put down her pen and joined Steve waiting to hear what else Coach had to say. He was uncharacteristically concise.

"Well? What are you waiting for? Come back and see me when you've bought your first property!"

17. Time for action

So, after some intensive coaching sessions Steve and Carol have learned a huge amount about property investment. Perhaps you already knew some of this? Maybe you could relate to our couple and their questions? You may even be looking for your own property coach! My hope is that, just like Carol and Steve, you now understand all the different topics and areas that a successful property investor must master. And, as we've heard throughout the book, there are *three* different routes you can follow as an investor:

1. Full-time: mastering each and every area and managing the entire operation yourself
2. Part-time: deciding which aspects to manage and which to leave to other people
3. Minimum-time: employing experts for all aspects.

Whichever route you choose, if you *understand* how it all works and you follow the rules, you will reap the benefits. But of course, unless you take your first step, nothing will happen!

The first step

What's the hardest thing for anyone contemplating something new? Is it fear of the unknown? Fear of getting it wrong, of failing? Or fear of discovering it was the wrong decision but there's no going back? Well, you don't need to have any of those holding you back. By observing Coach as he helped our couple adopt the mind-set of serious investors, you've already had a taste of what it's like but without making any commitment.

And the next step will keep you in this 'safety zone' for just a little longer, so don't panic!

I want you to immerse yourself in the world of property. There's no other way that you'll make the leap from these pages to building your own portfolio. It's hard work, but it's fun too! If you haven't already done this, look around your local area and find out about local property events. Remember PIN? Property Investor Network – look up www.pinmeeting.co.uk and you should find a group nearby. Or go onto our own website and see what events are coming up. There is a nominal attendance fee of £20 for monthly PIN events but if you input our promotional code "insight" you will be able to attend one for free. Whatever you do, get out there, meet as many other property investors as you can, talk to them and quiz them. The local knowledge they have is invaluable to you and will cost you nothing!

And don't forget the professionals – your core team of experts. You can be researching this right now; you'll need some of them in place and ready to move *fast* the moment you decide to buy your first property. Speak to lots of them – they are going to be key partners in your operation. Ask about their portfolios and ask to see the results they're getting in black and white. Make sure you feel completely confident in your final choice.

Remember, the only commitment you're making at this stage is to *find out more*, to discover if you are ready to seize this opportunity. If you're worrying about which of the three investor paths you're likely to follow, you can find out a lot more about the support and services from a company like mine at www.propertyinsight.info/learn/. Here you can watch videos and examine various documents and help pages. And if you decide that you want to have the peace of mind from employing experts to manage the process for you, look ahead to 'About our sponsors' which introduces the services of Property Insight.

Another section to read is chapter 20: Useful resources, where you can find all the websites and books that Coach mentioned during the sessions. These are all very useful sources of information which together cover every aspect of property investment. The websites of course are free to access and the price of the books is insignificant compared to what you can learn and the investment performance they can help you achieve.

Above all, however, I really want you just to take the next step. Your interest has brought you this far; hopefully Carol and Steve's experience has inspired you. And I will never get tired of explaining why this is such a fantastic way to invest now for a better future for you and your family. So, happy investing, good luck with your portfolio and good wishes for a prosperous future.

18. Our sponsors, Property Insight

Property Insight is a company with a vision – to directly help 4,000 families over the next 10 years to invest in property and become financially free. Achieving this means helping many more thousands of people to discover property investment and learn how a successful portfolio can lead to a fantastic financial future.

Founded on the experiences of the author, Aran Curry, the company has grown into a major provider of investment services and expertise. Key to its success is the ability to offer individualised support but always on the firm foundations of proven and highly successful investment models. For example, Property Insight helps clients to invest £60,000 which, over a ten year period, grows into a £1million portfolio with 25% equity. And this portfolio, based on a conservative 4% value increase, will deliver an annual tax-free and inflation-proof income of £30,000 year on year. This means that someone aged 30, starting today, will bring in this minimum income by the time they are only 40. Of course, some clients go on to invest multiples of £60,000, and it's not hard to work out the income that they enjoy!

However, results are only part of the picture. The other reason people who start with Property Insight stick with the business is peace of mind. The company covers all nine core competencies from sourcing the property below market value, negotiating, purchasing and financing, right through to refurbishment, tenanting and managing the tenancy. This means you can carry on with your life, reassured that real experts are using clear and proven rules to grow your portfolio for you.

The services are robust and well-tested. For example:

- Expert property purchase: the first three, bought in the first year, are guaranteed to be obtained for at least 15% below market value. This ensures that during this first year, 30% growth on the £60,000 investment is also guaranteed.

- Full management service: ensuring the properties are not just bought correctly, but refurbished, tenanted and managed expertly too.

Other innovative options include:

- Earning a 5% tax-free income on the £60,000 investment (a favourable alternative to interest on savings).

- Smaller portfolios, structured to deliver £20,000 a year (based on 4% growth).

And one particularly exciting option uses pensions to open up property investment to even more people:

- With pensions performing so poorly, many people would rather have the money invested in property under their control. By working with IFAs and SIPP Providers, Property Insight has found a way that clients can do this and make their pension work a lot harder.

So, Property Insight combines versatile and forward-thinking advice with comprehensive expertise in *all* the core competencies covered in this book. And this gives investors *confidence* – the confidence that their money will be made to work a lot harder, that the investment will be sound and secure, and that any or all aspects of managing their portfolio will be in safe hands.

What next?

Why not let us review your financial options and provide a FREE report showing how you could invest in your own portfolio in the months and years ahead?

To take advantage of this, please email aran.curry@ propertyinsight.info putting "Book Review" in the subject line. Or simply call us directly on 01723 506553 to find out how we can help.

You can review our full product range at www.propertyinsight. info/how-we-can-help/

"We unreservedly recommend everyone to talk to Property Insight before they make any investment planning."

"Aran's integrity, directness, commitment and concerned careful tailoring of his services to our needs are exceptional."

"Property Insight has over the last few months done exactly what they said they would do for me with masses of energy and enthusiasm and I have complete confidence in their recommendations and the work they do for me."

"No-one was more sceptical than us and no-one is now a greater supporter of Property Insight."

"In less than a year we have accumulated six properties and we joyfully and with great peace of mind are able to confirm the accuracy of his projections."

"Aran showed me a property investment opportunity several months ago; his presentation was very clear especially and any questions I had (and there were plenty) were answered very clearly and precisely which enabled me to make an informed decision on the investment."

"Reliable and forthright, Aran does what he says he will do. A rare quality in today's world."

"Aran is extremely knowledgeable about the residential property market from the point of view of investors. Coupled with his experience in the mortgage market, he provides very attractive investment packages to his clients. I look forward to working with him again in the future."

"I have worked with Aran on a number of Investment Property projects, and have also had the opportunity to listen to his presentations at his regular Property Seminars. I am always greatly impressed by his depth of knowledge in this area and his willingness to share the secrets of how he has made his Rental Properties work so successfully for him. I recommend him highly to anyone considering investing in this type of property."

19. Free bonus pack

Your Bonus Gifts worth £991

Simply log onto www.propertyinsight.info/bonusmaterial/ to claim these bonus items:

Free financial Review
Normally valued at £397, this review is carried out by one of Property Insight's expert advisors at our cost. With you, we review your current financial position and develop investment recommendations. The review helps you focus on areas to work on and where to go next in property.

Free Weekly Email from the Property Experts
Normal price £197, we offer you a short weekly video or written article that will increase your knowledge and skills in property. Eight different property experts have been involved in putting these emails together and we're proud to include them as a gift with this book.

Free Rental Pack
To add to the useful information found in chapter 13 (Managing Tenancies), we are offering this free pack (worth £97) with copies of tenancy agreements, procedures and documents for resolving tenancy problems. It also includes two free videos about maximizing your rents with LHA tenants, and a video showing how to be 98% occupied and 95% paid.

Discounted Mortgages

Our bonus pack includes a 61% discount on mortgage broker fees, worth £300. This means you pay only £195 for a buy to let expert to find you the best possible mortgage.

Property Investor Network attendance

Free entry to your first meeting of PIN anywhere in the country.

Go to www.propertyinsight.info/bonusmaterial/

Why do we give away so much free with the book? The answer is simple. We know from experience that when people get to know the business of the Insight Group and the expert work it does, they become clients and friends for life. And even for those who decide not to use us, if we have succeeded in sharing our passion for property investment and helped people to see its potential, then the book and the free extras have done their job.

---

20. Useful resources

Websites you will find useful

Tenancy documentation
PIMS, a website with every tenancy document you would ever need www.pims.co.uk

Local Housing Authority rents
Check what the local LHA rates are
https://lha-direct.voa.gov.uk/search.aspx (the address is sometimes changed so Google LHA rates if you have trouble finding the site)

Researching and valuing properties
Google earth: an internet search will lead you to a download for your computer
Net house prices: www.nethouseprices.com
Right move: www.rightmove.co.uk
Zoopla: www.zoopla.co.uk
Findaproperty: www.findaproperty.com

Credit checks
Experian: www.experian.co.uk
Equifax: www.equifax.co.uk

Great books to read
Rich Dad Poor Dad, Robert Kiyosaki
The Emyth Revisited – think of your investing as a business, Michael Gruber

Property Magic, Simon Zutshi

Make Cash in a Property Market Crash, *Rob Moore & Mark Homer*

The 44 Most Closely Guarded Property Secrets, *Rob Moore & Mark Homer*

Some useful Property Insight resources (www.propertyinsight.info)

Why invest in property www.propertyinsight.info/executive-briefing/

Free weekly videos www.propertyinsight.info/free-videos/

Other resources www.propertyinsight.info/keyrules/

Refurbishment www.propertyinsight.info/trafficlights/

Property Blog www.propertyinsight.info/blog/

Network magazine www.propertyinsight.info/ypn/

Mortgage brokers

Buy to let mortgage experts: www.mortgageinsight.co.uk

Letting agents

For the north-east: www.rentalinsight.co.uk

Other companies to help with your learning

Property Investing Network (PIN): www.pinmeetings.co.uk

Networking events

www.pinmeetings.co.uk or Google your town name + property event

Negotiating courses

Contact Rob Moore and his team at Progressive Properties http://www.progressiveproperty.co.uk/home/events/